SAVED FROM SILENCE

SAVED FROM SILENCE

✦

Amanda Richardson

iUniverse, Inc.
New York   Bloomington

SAVED FROM SILENCE

iUniverse books may be ordered through booksellers or by contacting:

iUniverse
1663 Liberty Drive
Bloomington, IN 47403
www.iuniverse.com
1-800-Authors (1-800-288-4677)

ISBN: 978-0-595-52444-0 (pbk)
ISBN: 978-0-595-51170-9 (cloth)
ISBN: 978-0-595-62498-0 (ebk)

Library of Congress Control Number: 2008941185

Printed in the United States of America

iUniverse rev. date: 2/13/2009

For Daniel, who has shown
me nothing but support for this journey. My daughter, who
gave me a reason to keep going. To my brother David,
my Aunt Mindy and Uncle David, Jesse, and Jeanell:
Thank you for teaching me unconditional love.
And to all those who prayed for
me along the way.

"It is essential that justice be done, and it is equally vital that justice not be confused with revenge, for the two are wholly different."

- Oscar Aria

Contents

Acknowledgments xiii

Preface... xv

Introduction... xvii

Chapter 1: Twenty-Four Hours 1

Chapter 2: Crying Out for Help 9

Chapter 3: Physical Pain, Emotional Suffering 17

Chapter 4: Revelations 25

Chapter 5: The Courage to Tell 33

Chapter 6: Coping with the Silence......................................41

Chapter 7: Confrontations 49

Chapter 8: Validation 61

Chapter 9: And the Bubble Bursts..69

Chapter 10: The Fire Spreads 79

Chapter 11: Tape Confessions 89

Chapter 12: Gift of Life 97

Chapter 13: Work in Progress..105

Chapter 14: Saying Good-Bye 115

Chapter 15: After Silence 125

Afterthoughts 129

Statistics 131

Helpful Resources 133

Additional Resources..135

Acknowledgments

To Cheri Laser and Paul Hawley – this book would have never become so amazing without your impressive editing skills. Your dedication and support with this project were remarkable. Thank you.

Angie—never underestimate your influence. Your prayers and support have undoubtedly played a role in my healing. I need more friends like you in my life.

Diana Walla—your patience is unmatchable. Your spirit loves. Your knowledge is healing. I can never thank you enough for all you've done for me.

Jennifer H.—you are a true friend. I can go months without seeing you and still feel as if you never left. You make me laugh at things that aren't funny, and you love me just the way I am. I love you.

Melinda Daniels—you are a rock. Thanks for always telling me the truth, even though I didn't want to hear it.

Lisa W.—you are truly an unsung hero. Always trust your instincts. You will never fully realize your influence in my life. Your mothering spirit kept me safe for many years.

Jesse and Jeanell—I could have never asked for better in-laws. Your guidance and wisdom have taught me how to live my life with dignity. I am truly blessed and better for having known you. You have taught me that some people are exactly who they appear to be.

I want to thank my incredible, brave, and wonderful husband, Daniel. Honey, you truly have given me strength when I've had none left in me. You are an impressive person. I am proud to have you by my side.

One hero in my life is definitely my brother, David. I can never tell you what your validation, support, and unconditional love have done for me. I thank you beyond words for your never-ending support. You inspire me to be the best I can be, and I could only hope that you will be as happy in your life as you deserve to be.

Aunt Mindy—you are also my hero. You are my hero in ways you will never be able to understand. You are far braver and stronger than I could have ever imagined.

And above all, I want to thank my patient, ever-loving, and healing God. Without my Savior, I am nothing. I have nothing. I can do nothing. My God is my eternal Father, my Redeemer, and the source of everything good I have in my life.

Preface

I first got the idea to write this book because so many people would ask me about my story. As the book evolved, I began to realize how actually reading the things that happened to me may affect people emotionally. For that, I apologize. But, in order for you to understand how I survived, you must know the events that I overcame.

I must also say that everything in this book is from my own opinion, my own personal thoughts, feelings, and memories. I am not professionally trained in mental health, and can only relate the things that impacted me personally and my journey past those things. This book is not intended to give medical or psychological advice, and readers should consult with professional counseling if needed.

My hope, however, is that my journey will be inspirational to others. Expanding awareness of what the silent epidemic of abuse is doing to our children and adult survivors is incredibly important. In my opinion, early intervention is a key element to recovery.

Many who read this book will either have been personally impacted or will be close to someone who has. For them, I would like to serve as a positive example of survival and recovery.

Other readers may find this to be their first exposure to a real story about the effects of child abuse. For them, I hope to impart a greater understanding and appreciation of the issue's depth and severity. There are multiple resources included in the back of the book for those who may need additional assistance.

I tell my story without shame, without the invitation for pity, and as candidly as I can, for the main purpose of aiding others but also to give a voice to the devastation of child abuse.

A widely used Christian phrase, the precise source of which is unknown, states that "you can't have a testimony without a test."

This is my testimony.

Introduction

Why do the smallest things sometimes cause such a great pain?

The maturity of the huge oak trees scattered across the country acreage where we lived harmonized with the landscape that lined the two lane highway leading to our property. The fifty acres we lived on were just outside of town and only a mile down New Harmony Road on the left side.

There was a curved hill that preceded our driveway and provided a perfect view of our family land and the four houses that lined the field. The dirt road that gave the only access to our house and two others was barely noticeable from the highway except for the large white sign that said "Tractor Repair" in cherry red letters. The numbers 525-4464 were printed at the bottom of the sign.

As you turned on the dirt road and rounded left around the first corner, our single-wide trailer house sat one hundred feet to the right in the middle of an open field. The blue paint that covered the cheap siding of our trailer was just a shade darker than a clear sky on a late spring day. But the maroon color of the trim created an odd look for the house and made our property appear even cheaper than it already was.

We parked our brown, '80s model, double-cab Ford F150 in the field in front of the house. Our trailer was placed just on the other side of a large drainage ditch that split our field in half. We placed a flat wooden bridge over the ditch so we could have an easy walkway to our front porch.

There were gray cinder blocks supporting the old planks that made up our steps and porch area. My brother and I spend countless hours on that porch, often playing childish games and picking fights with each other while we played.

There was something intriguing about those porch rails and my ability to swing on them, much in the same way we would swing from the branches of the oak trees. My little hands would rarely fail to drag across them in such a way that a tiny dagger would dig deep into my skin. Sometimes a splinter would find its way out without help, but rarely.

By appearance such a splinter would affect very little of me, but yet my mind would become etched with the unavoidable nuisance of the sting that had been created. The bit of wood that had pierced my skin had invaded my protective layer, with no effort. The longer I would let the irritant fester without taking any action, the deeper and more invasive the infection would become.

As I would look at my red, swollen skin, even in my adolescent mind, I knew that my body could not fight the infection on its own. Inevitably, I would resort to digging the splinter out, no matter how great the pain, because I knew that relief would not come if I did nothing.

Within the intense agony of that moment, as I poked and prodded the splinter to the surface, I hoped that hurting myself would result in a finger that felt better and an infection that would subside. Time and time again I succeeded.

As I've dragged myself through life, I've come in contact with more than my share of splinters, in both the literal and figurative senses. Some could pass my memory without an effort, but others daggered deep into my mind.

A woman asked me today how my father is doing, and without even thinking I responded indifferently and with as much politeness as I could muster. What a small exchange to cause so much pain. She invaded my protective layer, with no effort, and certainly no intent.

People often say that time will heal your pain, though surely time alone will not heal all pains. Sometimes you have to fight. Sometimes you have to cause yourself even greater pain in order to find relief. Allowing myself to be vulnerable to these human splinters is all a part of the final result: relief.

Time may not have healed my pain yet, but the hurt is certainly being revealed. And once that revelation is complete, all those memorial splinters that have accumulated throughout the years will work their way to the surface, without my having to dig at them any more.

Chapter 1

Twenty-Four Hours

ϒ

The sharp deafening sound of a loud intermittent tone jolts me from a light sleep.

Beep ... Beep ... Beep ... Beep.

It's 5:45 AM.

My feet hit the floor without hesitation, and already I am shaking from the intense rigidity I feel in every muscle of my little six-year-old body. The day starts with my stomach in knots, to the point that gagging is automatic but brings little relief.

"Hurry up. Get dressed," Momma whispers inside our doorway. "Y'all have thirty minutes. Hurry up." Her attempt to remain calm is quickly overshadowed by the anxiety that causes her voice to quiver.

Our trailer has only two bedrooms: my parents share one, and I share the other with my eight-year-old brother, David. Our bedroom is half filled with bunk beds where David sleeps on the top, and I sleep on the bottom.

The floor is covered by brown carpeting similar to the color of my dad's pickup outside, and the walls are made of laminate that mimics the appearance of wood paneling. The air is thick and musty, and the smell of fried grease lingers from supper the night before.

I grab a pair of folded jeans from our makeshift dresser made of crate boxes, and my mother comes to assist. She slips a T-shirt over my head and hands me a pair of socks.

"Come on. Let's do your hair," she says.

I leave the confines of my tiny bedroom and stand in front of the mirror in our bathroom where there is barely enough room for my mother to stand behind me. We look very different from each other. She has wavy fire-red hair that falls just at her shoulders and fair skin dotted with thousands of freckles. Her five-foot-three-inch frame is well proportioned, and her youth is still apparent despite the gray hair that has begun to appear on her late twenties head.

The top of my head falls several inches below her shoulders, and my long brunet hair and beige skin are an obvious contrast to hers. We do share the same sky blue eyes, and the hundreds of freckles that line my cheekbones give a clue to some of my heritage.

She quickly brushes my hair and leaves to check on my brother. I walk through the living room and grab my high-top sneakers from the closet just by the front door. I only recently learned how to tie them for myself.

It's six-o'clock. We have fifteen minutes. Loop … swoop … pull. Loop … swoop … pull.

My eyes are heavy: not like those of a sleepy child, but like those of a worn old man in a nursing home just counting the days until the fatigue does not plague him anymore.

I sit against the left arm of the couch dressed and ready for school, and my brother squeezes in right beside me. There is no doubt that he is my brother. He has the same brunet hair and beige skin, but he's much skinnier than me. I am on the heavy side of normal, and he's on the thin side. He can eat anything and never gain an ounce. He has the same freckles on his cheekbones, though not as apparent as mine. But his eyes are more hazel than blue.

He's sitting close enough to me that I can feel the crunch of his weight on my outer thigh, but the discomfort actually calms me, so I don't say anything. His closeness means more to me than the pinch.

My head sags onto my hand, which is propped on the arm of the couch, and I feel David's head fall onto my shoulder as he fails at fighting off the sleep himself.

"Please wake up, kids. Come on." My mom nudges us as she attempts to keep our attention. There is a sense of urgency in her movement, and her words have a distinct undertone of pleading.

She retreats to her bedroom to help my father get ready for work, and the silence becomes too tempting for my brother and me. Our eyes begin drifting slowly shut as the sound of *The Three Stooges* plays quietly on the television in the background. Several minutes elapse until we are abruptly awakened by the harsh sound of my father's baritone voice.

"Get up!" he yells at us.

The startle immediately sends throbs to my head, and my vision blurs with every heartbeat. He speaks like a person scolding a mutt dog who has trespassed into the yard.

We are expected to be ready and waiting for him at 6:15 sharp every morning. Seeing us asleep angers him because he considers our dozing to be lazy and disrespectful. He begins to yell and curse as he paces the floor, lecturing at us about our duties as his children, and I can feel the lump rising quickly in the base of my throat.

Please don't cry. Please don't cry. I swallow hard, trying to fight back the tears, but they roll down my cheeks despite all my efforts.

"You want something to cry about? Get up. I'll give you something to cry about. I'll teach you to disrespect me," my father says.

His face is red with fury, and when he speaks, the veins pop from his neck and forehead. He is a large man, well over six feet, and 230 pounds. His skin is swarthy and sun-kissed, with a slight leathery texture. His hair is dark brown, including his Southern man's mustache. He has broad shoulders, a little extra bulk around the waist, and small but muscular legs.

There is nothing I can do to reason with him or stop him from doing what he feels entitled to do. He takes his belt off and instructs me to pull my pants down. Mother pleads with him to stop, but her intrusion provokes him even further. He beats me with his belt, and the buckle cracks my skin enough to make me bleed.

Now I am awake.

My mother instructs me to "dry it up" and get to the truck, and I do just that, already learning how to conceal myself from the world. There is something about the smell of the truck when the motor is first cranked that I find calming, when the stale stench of old air hits you in the face. Finding comfort in such an aroma may sound like a peculiar thing, I suppose. But in many ways, that small play on my senses is my security blanket, because I always know that, at this point in my morning—even if for only thirty minutes—there will be calm.

I quickly put behind me the events of the morning and try to focus on the day ahead. Although my brother and I sit alone in the truck waiting, we speak not a word to each other. Each of us is just as scared as the other. But talking about our fear will only interfere with our denial, and hanging on to our denial is how we get through each day.

I'm sitting behind my father on the driver's side, slumped way down, with my head resting flush with the curved concave corner of the truck. I stare out the window, and I am soothed by the silence, which is heavy and tense but oddly safe. The only sound is the clutch spring squeaking as my father's foot presses the pedal to the floor.

We arrive at my father's work, and he exits the truck, carrying his lunch pail and walking hurriedly toward the entry gate. My mother slides over into the driver's seat, and I immediately sit up and begin squabbling with my brother about whose turn it is to sit up front. In an instant, we become ourselves.

"But you sat in the front yesterday," I announce.

"No, you did. It's my turn."

My mother allows this for several minutes before enforcing her wisdom. I win today, but not without a constant battle to elude David's hands, poking and pinching me from behind. As we arrive at school, my mother kisses us both on the cheek, tells us she loves us, and speaks those words that every mother says as her kids march off into the care of strangers: "Have a good day at school."

I try to focus on my schoolwork, but sitting in the hard plastic chair is painful because of the welts on the backs of my legs from earlier in the morning. I keep squirming in my seat, first putting one leg under the other, until that becomes too painful. Then I try to put my legs on the back of the wire rack in front of me. Nothing works.

As the day approaches three o'clock, my sweaty palms can't grip my pencil, and I feel faint. I begin to cry and am soon inconsolable. Every day around this time my stomach will turn and convulse in pain, and I often become physically ill.

My teacher helps me to the car and informs my mother about her concern for my health, suggesting that I may need to go see a doctor. Mother doesn't say much, only that she is aware of my stomach pains, and she will check into making me an appointment.

We pick up my father from work and head home. He is covered in black soot and smelly from the hours of sweat he produced in the heat, but he is quite affable and seems to have forgotten my earlier mistakes. He asks us about our day at school and takes an interest in listening to our stories. I tell him all about the things I learned, and my brother does the same. As we arrive at home, he reminds us of our chores and goes into the trailer to relax for the evening.

§

There is a small garden to one side of the trailer that contains a variety of vegetables. The sweltering East Texas summers enable our family to harvest enough food, and have plenty left over to preserve for the winter.

There is a shed, directly behind the garden, made of old wooden posts seven or eight feet tall and covered with tin along the top and backside. Inside there are three compartments: the first houses the lawn mower and other miscellaneous items; the second holds my father's tools; and the third and largest compartment shelters the chickens. There are at least ten chickens and sometimes twice that many.

David and I are responsible for many chores in the evenings. We tend the garden, keep the yard maintained, and gather eggs after feeding and watering the chickens amongst other things. Today is my day to attend to the chickens, and I have every intention of doing my best, but I am distracted by the overwhelming pressure that is building around my bladder.

I try to hold my bursting bladder for fear that using the bathroom before completing my chores may make Father mad. But as I proceed to the barn to begin my chores, the slow trickle of wetness begins to run down both legs.

What a loser. I'm so stupid.

I walk slowly back to the house, soaked in urine and crying in anger at myself for the lack of control.

I deserve whatever he gives me. How could I be so stupid?

I tremble as I walk in the door, and my mother escorts me to the bathroom where she cleans me up and gives me a change of clothes.

Hurry up.

Father is in the shower and blissfully unaware of these events. Mother reminds me to "dry it up" again and sends me back outside. Somehow, in the midst of all the drama, I forget to empty the chicken water and to put fresh corn in the trough. I return inside and take a bath and immediately begin my homework.

§

The smell of fried salmon patties fills the air and my stomach is growling in anticipation. I'm sitting in the living room, alphabetizing my spelling words for the week, when my father walks in from outside and slams the door.

"What's wrong with you? Why didn't you put fresh water in the chickens' trough?"

Do I tell him why I forgot or just take the punishment for forgetting? Which is worse?

"I don't know." I know my answer won't be acceptable, but I just don't know what to say.

"'I don't know' is not an answer. You have ten seconds to tell me why you didn't do your chores." He begins counting backward from ten. "Ten, nine … five, four, three …"

I make the decision to withhold my excuse, partly due to humiliation and partly because I'm afraid that my accident will just add to the punishment.

"I just didn't do them," I mumble.

He gets a glass from the cabinet above the sink and walks out the door. I know my punishment isn't over. He walks back in the house a few minutes later holding the same glass, only this time the glass is about three-fourths full of a murky liquid, particles floating throughout. He forces me to down a glass of dirty water from the chicken trough and sends me to bed without food, in an effort to "teach" me what the chickens felt like that evening. His tactic certainly works. I feel every bit as degraded and dirty as he intended me to.

I finally lay my head down, but my weary mind cannot relax with all the replay of events that circle in my head.

Please, God, keep me safe while I sleep. Help me be good tomorrow, and please don't let my daddy get mad at me. Please don't let the storms come during the night. Amen.

I am afraid to go to sleep for fear that my father will wake us up like so many times before, violent, with his belt in hand, to punish us for one of our many mishaps he had failed to catch earlier in the day. Or that he will decide, once again, that 2:00 AM is a good time to clean the house. I am so tired, but afraid to sleep. So I lie there, hour after hour, and at last glance the clock reads 1:00 AM.

The sharp deafening sound of a loud intermittent tone jolts me from a light sleep.

Beep … Beep … Beep … Beep.

It's 5:45 AM.

Chapter 2

Crying Out for Help

ɤ

I have spent the majority of my life living in what I refer to as "the bubble." The bubble has many layers, and reality does not exist inside the bubble. Part of the bubble was created for me, made out of the frame of reference by which I came. But much of the bubble I made for myself, to protect myself from reality, and also to protect me from myself.

Living inside a bubble means that all external interactions are clouded by the haze that forms the bubble. Every conversation, every contact, and every relationship is altered because there is no real perception.

The very nature of a bubble suggests that it cannot last forever. My bubble began to disintegrate in January of 2005.

I walked into the office of my nurse practitioner, Janet, for a routine annual physical. I had no idea how this meeting would change my life. I filled out my medical update and checked "yes" beside the question about depression.

I had taken the time that morning to first straighten my hair, still long and brunet, and then curl the ends until my hair fell just lower than my shoulders. My makeup was perfect. The faded freckles on my cheeks were concealed beneath foundation and pink blush. And my blue eyes were highlighted well with black liner and thick mascara. I kept my 145-pound frame hidden beneath a black knee-length trench coat. My low self-esteem was easier to comfort during the winter when full body clothing was socially acceptable.

Janet walked into the exam room, still reading my chart, then quickly sat down in front of me and removed her glasses.

"I see you've checked 'yes' beside depression," she said.

I couldn't help but feel as though making that checkmark had been a mistake. "Yeah, I just kind of feel sad sometimes. It's not really a big deal. I just think I have a little depression. Maybe I need some medicine or something."

I desperately wanted to sound convincing, to downplay the intense emotions that I was experiencing. But as I sat there saying such casual and deflective responses, my body began to shake with uncontainable anxiety.

"Are you happy with your marriage?" she asked.

"Very happy. I really don't think it has anything to do with my marriage."

"What about your job?"

Shut up already. I obviously don't want to talk about it.

"No, my job is going fine. I'm pretty sure it isn't that either." I could feel the awkwardness in the air, and I felt the need to fix it. "I'm just depressed. I don't really know why. I've been depressed off and on for a long time. To be honest with you, I had some problems with abuse in my childhood, but I really don't want to talk about it. Besides, I think I am past that, so…"

"I understand. I'll be happy to give you a prescription, but I want to encourage you to see a counselor. That could really help you figure out where the depression is coming from. I don't feel comfortable just giving you the medicine without having you talk to someone."

"All right. I mean…I really don't need to talk about it, but I guess I'll go.

"I know an excellent counselor. Her name is Diana Walla. I want you to go see her. You don't have to talk about the abuse if you don't want to. We just need a third party to help us with evaluating how well the medicine works for your depression. It'll take several weeks before you even notice any changes. Will you make an appointment with Diana and at least meet her?"

"I will. I'll give it a try."

I left the office that day in complete despair, literally wrecked with anxiety and feeling hopeless. I was angry at myself for revealing my depression to her, and I wondered how I was going to make it through a counseling session and convince the therapist that this was all a waste of time.

Despite these misgivings and my second-guessing, I followed Janet's advice and called Diana Walla. I set up an appointment with her, advising her I would only be coming in at Janet's request, and reluctantly went to my first appointment.

Her office was located in the middle of town, about a twenty-minute drive from my house. I had plenty of time to rethink my decision before I arrived.

How am I going to talk to this woman for fifty minutes?

I parked my car facing the road and walked slowly toward the glass door just underneath the number one, which signaled that I was entering the proper building. Her waiting room was the first room straight ahead as I walked through the entrance. The gentle rumble of an air conditioner helped drown out noise from adjacent rooms.

There were two straight-back chairs on the right wall, separated by a round side table that held various magazines on its glass top. But I chose to sit on the couch that lined the wall immediately to the left of the doorway. From that day forward, I would always sit in the same spot, as close to the left arm of the couch as my body would allow. This sitting position was a habit I had carried over from my childhood.

I was sitting in the waiting room holding an accent pillow in my lap to try and relieve myself from feeling that I would puke. My internal dialogue was continually self-destructive.

This is all a big mistake. I shouldn't be here. I should just leave. I don't need the medicine anyway. She doesn't even care. She's not going to get it. I don't need sympathy. I'm just crazy. That's all. I'm crazy, and I need medication.

"Amanda? Hi. I'm Diana Walla."

"Hi. It's nice to meet you." I stood up and shook her hand with my cold, clammy palm.

"Nice to meet you too. Follow me. My office is around the corner."

She made small talk, asking me about the weather and my ability to find her office.

Wow, she's really nice. She isn't treating me like a patient. I'm not a patient. I'm an adult. I don't even need her. I was searching for any reason to make this not work out.

She was a tall woman, probably standing close to six feet, with a great figure, middle-aged, with dirty blond hair that fell just above her shoulders. She was dressed professionally, but with a casual tinge, and she wore very little makeup. I immediately found her to be kind, tender, and—most important—approachable.

"Have a seat. So, Janet referred you to me?" She wasted no time getting down to business.

Here we go.

"Um, yeah. When I went in for my annual, I told her I was depressed, and she gave me some medicine and said I needed to see someone to help regulate the medicine. That's all."

"So what kind of goals would you like me to help you meet?"

Isn't that the million dollar therapy question?

"Well, I guess just to get to the point where I don't feel so depressed. I do want to be honest with you. I have had lots of things in my past that I am pretty sure are causing some of my depression, but I don't need to talk about it because it's kind of behind me."

Shut up. What are you doing?

"Okay."

Okay? Aren't you going to ask me something else, something more invasive?

There was a long silence after her brief response. I felt very uncomfortable and, again, gave in to my impulse to fill the empty air.

"I have a wonderful husband and a great job, so I don't see why I should be depressed. I can hardly even get out of the bed in the mornings. I feel like there is no use for me to even start the day. It is overwhelming at times. I feel guilty, though, like I shouldn't be depressed, but I just can't shake it. I have tried and tried, and I cannot shake this depression by myself. It seems to be getting worse. That's why I decided to tell Janet, so maybe I can get some medicine, and it will help."

"What kind of medication did she start you on?"

"Paxil." *Paxil, Zoloft, Wellbutrin. What's the difference?*

"And how long have you been on it?"

"Probably about two weeks, but it isn't helping."

"Well, it can take up to six weeks before you notice a difference. Why don't you tell me a little about yourself?" she said, changing the subject.

Ha! That's funny. You don't want to know a little about me. If you could see inside my head right now, you'd probably run the other way.

"Okay. Um, well, I'm twenty-three years old. I've been married for about a year and a half, and I am a hygienist. I have lived on my own since I was eighteen, and I put myself through college. I dated my husband for four years before I married him, and we have a great relationship. That's why I can't figure out why I am depressed. I have a lot going for me. We just bought our first house about six months ago, and we both have good jobs. There really isn't anything for me to be depressed about."

Ramble a little more, why don't you?

"Do you have any theories as to why you might be depressed?"

Theories? Oh I have more than theories, lady. I'm crazy. I'm messed up. I'm really screwed up. Everything I do is a facade. I'm fake, and I've been fake my whole life. I don't know who I am or why I'm here. I am a fake person. Everything I do and say is fake, fake, fake, fake!

"Not really. Like I said, everything is going good for me."

"Well, you said there were some things in your past that could be causing your depression."

"Well, yeah, but just like childhood stuff, you know. But I don't know why it would cause me to be so depressed today. I should be happy for everything that is going well."

What do you people not get about the fact that I don't need to talk about my freaking childhood? Everything is fine today.

"I really don't think I need counseling, but I told Janet I would come and talk to you because she didn't feel comfortable giving me the medicine without someone else helping to see how well it's working."

We continued with mindless chatter for a while and, before long, she was closing our session—elegantly, I might add, with her electronic scheduler in hand. She didn't close the hour at all like I had imagined she would. There wasn't a clock ticking and a buzzer sounding at the end of the fifty minutes.

No, she simply picked up her scheduler and began making me another appointment.

"I'd like to see you again next week—you know, to check on your progress and see if the medication is helping."

"Okay, I can do that. It is kind of nice just to get things off my chest sometimes."

"That's what I'm here for. You can vent anything to me."

I left her office feeling the truth behind her statement. She really seemed to listen to me. From the very beginning, I felt comfortable with her. Our weekly sessions continued, and I began to feel the medication help ease my constant, chronic anxiety. In turn, speaking to Diana became easier for me. Those early sessions were an integral part of my therapy, just learning to trust Diana and building a relationship with her. Our pointless chatter continued for a while, and I continued to maintain my denial. Many sessions would pass before I would begin to reveal the true nature of my depression.

Chapter 3

Physical Pain, Emotional Suffering

♈

I can never remember feeling at peace as a child. I was always worried about what I would do wrong, or how I would disappoint my father—mostly because I knew I would. Making him mad didn't ever take much. He always felt the need to exert his control over us, even in the most trivial of situations.

Though people knew he had a propensity to be hard on us, he managed to keep his true nature hidden very well. Of course, we knew how to behave when we were around other people. Such adaptability was innate. There is no manual for children living with child abuse. Most of the behavior evolves as a matter of protection.

People will often ask, "Why didn't they tell?" But I tend to think, *Why would they tell?* Children know only the moment they are in. They aren't capable of predicting the impact of their actions beyond the basic needs of survival. Children are hardwired to survive.

Of course I *wanted* to tell, but *what* would I tell? How much of what was happening was not normal? How was I to know? If I told, what would happen to me when I got home? What would my father do to me?

Thinking in terms of an immediate threat, all I could do was try to protect myself and play along with the image. So that was exactly what I did. I adapted. We played a good game.

By all appearances, we were the perfect family. Sure, we were poor, but everyone was poor in the '80s.

There weren't many trees covering the field where our trailer sat, so summers were excruciatingly hot. Though torturous at times, the heat and humidity did create a perfect environment for gardening. We grew a little bit of everything in that garden. It was approximately fifty feet long and seventy-five feet wide and was split into at least ten rows. There were several rows of potatoes and onions, lots of tomato vines, and all the squash, okra, and cabbage a family could possible need.

My father often used the garden as a means of punishment. The loneliest times were when only one of us got into trouble. I often secretly wished that David would get into trouble too, just so I didn't have to endure my punishment alone. Selfish as my wishes may sound, David's presence always brought me a lot of comfort.

I can still feel the dirt underneath my fingernails from picking the blades of grass, one by one, out of the garden. Sometimes this would last for hours, or even all day, depending on the degree of punishment my father felt we deserved. My fingers would be stained green and the dirt would wedge so deeply into my nails that cleaning them later was impossible, even with a file. My knees would be caked with dirt from bending down for so many hours, and my hair would be soaked in sweat. If he was really mad at us, we would have to pick the grass out of the garden without bending down on our knees. If there was dirt on our knees, the belt would follow.

I really hated that garden.

My father was not only stern with us. He had a way of degrading us down to our core. He made me feel so much shame about the person I was, and the person I was to become. Some of my earliest memories are of him telling me how fat I was and how nobody would ever like me if I was fat and ugly. I was probably in the second grade the first time he put me on a diet. I remember my mother sneaking me food when he wasn't around.

I truly believed in what he told me at the time. I thought I was disgusting, because he thought that I was. No matter how many people would stop and tell me I was pretty, their compliments simply did not sink in. Surely they were just lying to me to make me feel better about myself, because my dad had already told me the truth.

§

There was one day that I will never forget. I was probably eight years old. The day was smoldering and hot, and I was once again in trouble. I cannot remember what I did wrong that day, only the events that followed.

Beside the shed, on the left side, sat a pile of old cardboard boxes. I assumed they were placed there when we moved several years before because they had been there as long as I could remember. Over several years of rain and sun exposure, the boxes had somehow become one big pile of slimy rot. My punishment that day was to take the boxes to the burn pile and make the side of the shed look good again.

"Don't come into this house until all the boxes are gone. I don't want to come out there and find a bad job. I want it to look good. I don't care how long it takes."

I began working sometime around noon. The tears and sweat rolled down my face simultaneously. The boxes were nothing but mush, and every layer contained more green slime than the last. And not just green, but dark, decay-tinted green. They were disgusting. He wouldn't allow me to use anything but my hands.

The day was long and seemed to drag on forever. I was covered in green gunk, and I gagged at the smell of my own putrid odor. The sun began to set, and I decided to drag my task out even further, hoping that I could just go inside and take a bath and do my chores without having to face him again.

"Hurry up!" he yelled from the porch. "You have thirty minutes."

I had already finished, but I didn't want him to know that. Any amount of time I could spend away from him lessened my chances of screwing up again. About thirty minutes later, he came to inspect my job. He walked over, took a look at the job I'd done, and then turned away saying, "Let's go."

"Where are we going?" I asked.

"To the store."

"But I'm dirty. Can I please take a bath first?"

I reeked. Not just of the old slimy boxes but of hours of perspiration. My clothes were feculent and my hair was in shambles. He didn't say a word about the hard work I had put in that day. He began walking away and turned his neck just enough for me to hear him say, "Nope. We're going to town. And you're going just like that, so everyone can see how filthy you are."

I began to cry of embarrassment.

"Dry it up, or I'll give you something to cry about." That was one of his famous lines. Granted, that phrase is used by many parents to motivate their children, but he took the words literally.

Our drive to the store was silent. My brother rode in the front seat, and I was in the back, behind my father where I usually rode. We were going to the store to pick out a movie.

Maybe he'll let me stay in the truck, I thought.

"Come on, kids," he said when we arrived at the store. "You too," he added, looking straight at me.

"I don't want to …"

"I *said,* come on," he interrupted.

We walked into the store, and he began searching for a movie to rent. People were staring at me in disgust, and he took notice.

"Go stand over there until I'm done. I don't want people to know you're with me. You stink."

I walked to the corner of the store and stood there waiting for him to finish. People were staring and commenting under their breath. I was exhausted from all the hard work I'd done that day, but I no longer felt the achiness in my muscles. I felt only humiliation. I was worthless, and this experience proved my insignificance even more. I was nothing but a bad kid who was filthy and smelly, and nobody else would want me. That I knew for sure.

I don't remember anything else from that evening. I'm sure I went home and bathed and continued things as normal, but I have no recollection of those events—only the shame I had experienced.

§

As hard as my father was on me physically, he was even harder on my brother. He seemed to take delight in hitting my brother in the head and calling him stupid. My brother definitely took more physical beatings than I did.

"Go get a peach tree limb from the orchard. You have three minutes," he'd say. "For every minute you're late, that will be another lick."

The peach orchard was toward the back of the property and impossible to reach in three minutes. He would give David this infeasible task and set him up for failure. Every time he would make my brother get a peach tree limb I would nearly get sick. I felt sorry for David. I wanted to take half of his punishment, so he wouldn't be alone. My father always made sure that, if one of us was in trouble alone, the other was standing right there to see the penalty. I felt helpless. All I could do was stand there and watch him get beaten.

The most terrifying beating that David took was not actually the worst one. My father was extremely quick tempered. He would be fine and smiling one minute and literally swinging at us the next. There was no way to predict his anger. We were outside working in the garden, and my father asked me to go inside and get him a glass of iced tea. As I approached the house, I could hear my father's voice getting louder in anger. He got mad so quickly.

"How could you be so stupid?" he would always say to David.

There was a big bay window in the kitchen that faced the garden area. I poured his tea and looked out the window at my father standing directly over my brother, intimidating him. My brother stood frozen solid. I could see the fear in his face, even from all that distance. I walked out on the porch and heard my brother screaming.

"No, please don't. Daddy, please."

My father had grabbed the first thing he could get his hands on, which was his saw—three feet long with a wooden handle and rusty teeth. He pulled back his arm as far as he could reach and began beating David with the saw. I screamed in horror and cried, running toward them with my father's tea spilling all over my arm.

"Please stop, Daddy, please." I was crying.

I thought in that moment that he was going to kill my brother. I literally stood horrified at the fact that David was about to be sawed in half. David stood bent half over, holding onto the wooden saw table, with my father steadily swinging the saw at him. All the while, David kept screaming at our father to stop, and tears streamed down his little face, making streak marks in the layer of muck underneath. As I approached with my father's glass of tea, he stopped swinging, took the glass of tea, threw the saw to the ground, and told us to continue working. As quickly as the terror had erupted, the incident was over.

I wanted to hug David. I wanted to tell him that everything was okay. More than that, I wanted to take the fear away from his eyes. But I couldn't. He put his head down, and I did the same, and we continued to pick grass from the garden. David and I would not speak of that horrifying episode again until our adulthood.

Chapter 4

Revelations

ɤ

About six weeks had passed since I started therapy, and it was early March of 2005. I knew on the inside that I desperately needed to talk about what had happened to me, but my internal dialogue left me feeling insecure and doubtful. Although my sessions with Diana had begun to reveal small pieces of my past that I had previously kept well hidden, the mental turmoil I felt about what to do and say next was excruciating.

Am I going to come across as whiny? Will she even believe me? I cannot continue to go on like this. It's now or never.

All I could think about was how torturous every encounter in my daily life had become and how keeping my secrets locked up was starting to affect every aspect of my life.

What if it's not a big deal? What if I am overreacting and she tells me that I need to find a way to get over it?

I gradually began to disclose the physical and mental anguish I had endured. But I knew I was just skimming the surface, and so did Diana. Every time I thought I was ready to open up to her, my tongue would freeze, and my inner thoughts would stop me.

It could've been worse, I'd tell myself. *There's nothing she can do to help me anyway.*

At that early point, though, I wasn't sure how much of what had happened to me qualified as abuse rather than actions that fell within normal ranges of parenting and discipline. But I was confident that my father had crossed some sort of line and had done things he shouldn't have.

By this time, I'd been seeing Diana for probably six weeks and struggling through at least a half a dozen sessions where the words began fighting to get out. I had believed for some time that I would probably end up telling her everything, eventually. Unbeknownst to me, though, all the years of festering pressure and anguish were coalescing like a rotting ulcer and preparing to explode.

The session in question didn't start out as anything special. But I was unaware that this was going to be *the* day, the one where God would give me the courage to unburden myself, the one that would set in motion the chain of events that would ultimately free me from my bubble.

I wanted to warn her. I felt like I had to protect her from what she was about to hear. "There is so much I want to tell you," I heard myself say to her, "but it is so deep and embarrassing, and I don't know if I can even get it out."

"There is no embarrassment in this room. There is nothing you can tell me that won't be safe."

"I know, but it's really hard. I don't think you understand."

"Take your time."

"Okay. Well, there was this day that I remember. It still feels like yesterday."

I really don't know how to tell you this.

"I ... I don't really know where to start," I stuttered.

"Take a deep breath. You can do it," she encouraged. "Just say the words however they come out."

"I was about ten years old. I remember that I was out of the fifth grade and going into the sixth grade. It was around the Fourth of July because my brother was going with the youth group to pop fireworks, and I wasn't old enough to go with him."

God, please help me.

"Give me a minute. I just need a minute. I'm sorry."

"Don't be sorry. Take as long as you need."

"My memory starts with me lying on my father's bed. I'm sure he called me into the bedroom, but I don't remember that part. He would always call me into the bedroom and shut the door to make me rub his back."

I paused and put my head down between my legs. I was shaking all over and feeling my heartbeat in my head.

"I don't know if I can do this."

"Yes, you can. Take your time."

"Give me just a minute. I feel sick."

"Take a deep breath. It's okay. Take as long as you need."

"We hadn't been in there very long. He asked me to pull my shirt up so he could 'examine' me. He told me he was my father, and he had the right to see if I was developing properly. That's when he started to molest me. The tears were rolling down my cheeks, and he just kept doing it. He had this look in his eye. It was evil. I know that sounds strange, but I don't know any other way to explain it. It was pure evil. I felt like I could only see a part of him, and the rest was just possessed. I really didn't understand what was happening to me."

As I sat there in Diana's office, my words were increasingly jumbled and partially incoherent. My hands were grabbing my hair, and my head was hung in shame.

"It's okay."

Oh, God … please help me.

"I don't think you understand. This is really hard to talk about."

"You're doing well. Just breathe slowly, and take your time."

My mind took me right back to that moment, flashing in reverse with clarity, as if the event had happened only minutes before.

"He kept asking me questions, and I was just lying there crying, but he still did it anyway. My brother knocked on the door and told my father he was leaving. I was in shock. I just felt numb. I could see what he was doing, but all the sounds were muffled. I felt like I was standing beside the bed watching it happen to someone else. I remember I was wearing my favorite pink pants that day, and the covers were hanging halfway off the end of the bed. The bathroom door was halfway open, and the light from the bathroom window seemed so bright."

Diana just sat and listened to me.

"I remember him telling me to put my clothes back on and then getting ready for work himself. He had a job at a grocery store at that time, and he had just been made the employee of the month."

Employee of the month!

"How messed up is that? He told me this was our secret and that all fathers did this with their daughters. He told me that my mother didn't need to know because she wouldn't understand. They had been having problems anyway, and this would just confuse her. He didn't even have to tell me all that. I knew not to tell. I was afraid of him. There was this look in his eye that told me he could kill me and feel no remorse."

Being in Diana's office always felt like a continuation of the previous session. When I would talk, my eyes seemed to focus where the left wall met the ceiling, and on the flaws in the cool cucumber paint job she had most likely done herself. Not that they were noticeable flaws. She did a great job decorating with red and black accents, and the beige color of her suede couch helped bring a modern feel to the room. But looking at her face while I spoke felt uncomfortable, and focusing in on the minor slips of paint I saw kept me from having to look her in the eyes.

"I don't remember at all what I did that afternoon. It was like I lost time. I think I was in shock all day. I wanted to tell my mom so bad, but I knew I couldn't. I just couldn't do it."

"So what happened after he went to work?" she continued.

"The next thing I remember is being in the car on the way to the store still in shock and thinking about what had happened. I had the strangest emotional reaction with my mother. I was faking being in a good mood to the point that it was strange. She even asked me why I was in such a good mood. I just kept thinking, *Oh, if you only knew*. And I remember feeling really hot, like I actually ran a fever because I was so nervous during that car ride. It was so strange."

See, I told you I was crazy. Oh God, I can't believe I just told you that. What was I thinking? I'm not thinking. I can't think. Please help me. Please…someone help me.

"You're okay. You did well."

"Am I crazy? 'Cause sometimes I think I'm crazy."

"There is one thing I do know. You are definitely not crazy. You are so far from crazy, it's a miracle."

"Yeah. But there is so much more. Like if you knew everything, you'd definitely think I'm crazy. I have this ability to completely dissociate from myself. I can go to work for a whole day and not even remember what I did. It's like I'm on autopilot all the time. That's crazy."

"I know enough to know you're not crazy. First of all, people who are crazy usually don't know they are. Second, the way you are responding is very normal in an abnormal situation. Do you understand what that means?"

"Not really."

Her appearance was always meticulous, with clean, pressed blouses and straight-legged pants. She was tall enough that sitting in her chair with her legs crossed made even her longest dress slacks pull above the ankle.

"Sometimes people do things and act in certain ways in response to things that have happened to them," she reassured me. "There is a lot of documentation about abuse and how people respond to it, and one thing we have learned is that there are normal responses to abuse. And two of those responses are dissociation and denial. The way you describe your feeling of an 'out-of-body' experience is a very normal reaction to the sexual abuse you were experiencing."

"I was devastated. I mean, I knew that my father had been abusive, but this was different. In a single moment, he changed who I was."

"And did this continue?"

"Oh, he didn't stop. He started coming into my room at night and trying to feel of me while I was sleeping. I would wear my bra to bed and sleep with my arms tucked in close beside me to try and deter him. He even took the locks off the bathroom door, so he could walk in on me while I was showering. I felt like I lost all my privacy. I really lost who I was. He made me feel like I was in prison."

Though I was pouring my heart out, purging as I would call it, I knew that just talking about the abuse was not going to help. My real problem was the bubble. I couldn't stand living my life in the bubble. I was slowly suffocating, and I knew if I didn't escape, I would die in the bubble.

See, living my life in the bubble felt like I was trapped inside someone else's world. I knew that somewhere inside me there was still a real person desperate to live her own life. People say that life is a stage, but every day inside the bubble was like acting in someone else's play. Everything I said, did, and felt was scripted by someone else. My parents wrote my script for me. But in order for me to get out of the bubble, I knew I would have to purge as well.

"Did most of the abuse happen while you were sleeping?"

"No. The bad stuff always happened in the mornings before school or before my brother would wake up. That's when he would call for me to come into his bedroom.

"Was your mom there?"

"No, no, no. She left for work at like 5:30 every morning. That's why he did it in the mornings. Sometimes I would pretend to still be asleep or act like I couldn't hear him, but he would keep calling my name louder and louder until I came. There was a certain tone in his voice when I could tell he was getting mad, and I knew I had to go."

"Do you understand that it is all 'bad'? There really is no good and bad sexual abuse."

"Well, intellectually I understand. I understand a lot of things intellectually. But the way I feel about them doesn't always match. In my mind, I felt the need to separate the 'good' and the 'bad' things. It made it easier; I guess it minimized it a lot. Does that make sense?"

"Of course it does."

I was still shaking, but able to speak clearly. I could feel our session winding down.

"My mom had to know something wasn't right. I let my physical appearance deteriorate to the point that other kids would make fun of me. I gained about thirty pounds. I became such a different person. I was angry all the time, and I fought with my mom a lot. My parents told me all the time that I had an attitude problem. I probably did. I hated everything and everybody."

"Why do you think your appearance slipped so drastically?"

"Well, I'd guess it was probably some kind of subconscious effort to repulse him, but I sure didn't know it at the time."

"I have to tell you … you really seem to have a lot of insight."

"Yeah. You're right, I do. But it still doesn't make me feel any better. I can't stand the fact that I still have to pretend. The fact that nobody knows what he really is. And I can't stand sitting across from him at Thanksgiving dinner, pretending to have the perfect family. It's eating me alive."

She pulled out that scheduler a little over an hour after our session began.

"I really feel like you made a lot of progress today. I'm proud of you. I know that was hard, but you did well."

Progress? You call this progress? I call it a disaster. You actually want me to come back. Are you a glutton for punishment?

"There is a book ... well, actually two books that I would like you to read. I really think they will help you get your thoughts out. One is called *Toxic Parents*, and the other one is *The Courage to Heal.* I would really like you to start with *Toxic Parents*. I think it will be very insightful for you and help you to figure out the difference between normal and abusive. Will you read it?"

Will I read it? Of course I'll read it. I don't think you understand how desperate I am. I'm dying here. How are you not completely disgusted with me?

"Yes, of course. I'll go buy it today."

She gave some final thoughts and brought the session to a close.

"Great. And I'll see you next week. If you need anything at all, please call me. If you need to come and talk before our appointment next week, let me know. I'm here for you. I mean that."

"Okay. I'm sure I'll be okay. I'll see you next week."

Chapter 5

The Courage to Tell

ϒ

My mother is the queen of denial. She always has been, and she has always managed to create a sense of normalcy, even in the face of extreme distress.

I was about fourteen the first time I told my mother what was happening to me. Granted, the confession didn't exactly come out as I am telling the story now.

My father began working at the local tire factory when I was eleven. Twenty dollars an hour was an excellent salary back then, especially considering the insurance and benefits that he received. Our trailer had begun rapidly deteriorating, so when the home directly in front of us was put up for sale, my parents jumped at the opportunity to buy.

I had the bedroom furthest away from my parents' room, though the distance didn't seem to deter my father at all. The early morning sun beamed through my bedroom window with such freshness that day that the tragedy ahead was unforeseeable.

I remember that day as if it happened yesterday. My father had been abusing me for many years, and I had reached a point of such hatred and anger toward him that I literally could not stand his behavior any longer.

David wasn't home that day, and my father began calling out my name out as usual. I ignored him. He continued to call out my name, getting angrier each time he called. I continued to ignore him.

Finally he came down the hallway and asked, "Can't you hear me calling you? Come on."

Of course I can hear you, I thought. *What? Am I deaf? Isn't it obvious that I hate you? Isn't it obvious that I clearly don't want to come or I would have already?*

I stepped into the hallway as he turned and headed back toward his bedroom. He still had morning hair going in every direction, and he hadn't even bothered to put on a shirt. He wore only a pair of thin red cotton shorts that fell just above his knees. They were the kind of shorts that had a thick elastic band around the waist and two poorly sewn pockets on either side. He had these same discount store shorts in every color available.

I followed him into the bedroom, extremely nervous. I was hot again. I was feverish with anger. Over the years, I had perfected the ability to numb myself, to lose time, as if there were two of me—the abused and me. I hated the abused. I hated her because she was unable to make him stop. I detested her because she was ugly and fat and no good.

Not today. He's not going to do this to me today.

"I don't want you to do this," the abused mumbled, not quite as bold as I had wanted her to be.

"What did you say to me?" He was surprised.

"I said *no!* I don't want you to do this anymore." This time I declared my objection. I hadn't spoken with that much passion in my voice in a long time, if ever.

"Did you just say no to me?" He was enraged. The look in his eye sent fear through my body. I saw the same evil I had seen many times before, but this time the evil was combined with fury. Every ounce of my being was telling me I should have kept quiet, but the words had come from somewhere else, somewhere I wasn't used to. I was no longer acting for myself. My body took over—my "fight or flight" response, as they say. My body said fight *and* flight.

I tried to get away from him, but he was twice my size. He had me pinned down on all fours. His legs held my legs and his hands squeezed the underside of my forearms as they lay beside my head. He pressed so tightly on my arms that I could feel my fingers tingle as they began to fall asleep.

Oh God … He's gonna kill me … Oh God.

We were all alone in that bedroom. Nobody would hear me scream, and nobody was coming to rescue me.

I pleaded with him, "Stop … Please … don't… Please, I'm begging you. Don't."

This is it. He's gonna strangle me right here and hide my body, and nobody will ever know. Somebody please help me.

But there wasn't anyone there.

"Stop yelling at me. You don't tell me no. I'll teach you to tell me no."

God, please.

I mustered all my strength and said a quick prayer. I remember closing my eyes and trying to roll out from under his strength, and somehow, I opened my eyes standing on the side of the bed. He was standing at the end of the bed facing me. I had never seen him look that furious.

He's gonna kill me. There's no way for me to escape. He is going to kill me. If I run for the door, he'll catch me before I can get out of it. God, please help me. Please. Either let him kill me, or get me out of here. I can't stand it any longer. I'd rather die. I would.

"Please think about this. Please just calm down and think about this. You don't want to do this. Whatever it is you're thinking, you don't want to do it," I begged him.

God, please ... please help me.

I could see the evil in his eye begin to calm. I felt as if someone had flipped a switch, and somehow something I was saying to him finally got through. He slowly walked around the bed and sat down facing me. He took a few moments to gather his composure and immediately began his attempt to justify what had just happened.

"I know this looks bad, but it probably isn't what you thought. I wasn't going to hurt you. I would never do anything to hurt you. You know that, don't you?"

Are you kidding me? Haven't you done enough?

"Yeah, I know." I would have said anything in that moment just to get him to calm down.

"Go to your room. Don't speak about this to anyone. Do you understand?"

I just nodded and left the bedroom. Only this time, I was going to make him stop. I could feel in my bones that he could have killed me earlier in the day. I really could feel in the core of who I was that I was going to die. All the events of that morning seemed to pass in slow motion, with our voices muffled. Time was drastically slower, and I could not control the actions of my body. There was something in my soul that sensed immense danger and took control for me. I felt like I had just witnessed my own murder. As quickly as he had stopped, he could have ended my life.

In my mind, if I didn't tell, I believed that the next time he would kill me. I was terrified. I was afraid for the safety of not only myself, but my mother and brother as well. He was crazy. I either had to tell or run away.

But I didn't think I had anywhere to run. Nobody knew how he was. To everyone who knew us, he was a loving, attentive father and a supportive husband. We attended our church regularly, and I was active in the youth group. I was even best friends with our youth minister's daughter.

There were times that my father abused me on Sunday morning and then took me to church. Nobody had any idea. They would all think I was crazy. In my mind, my mother was the only one capable of protecting me.

My father left for work around three, and my mom arrived home around that same time. Several hours passed before I could work up the nerve to tell her what had happened earlier that day. I really didn't even know what to say. I didn't think I could actually speak those words.

Acknowledging the abuse to her meant I had to also admit this tragedy to myself. I am still not sure why it is so hard to utter the words of abuse to another person. In many ways, telling her about the abuse seemed more difficult than enduring it.

As a child, I had found a way to blame myself. If only I'd been better, if I'd been more thorough with my chores, if I could make their marriage happier, then maybe he wouldn't do this to me. But the harder I tried, the more I failed. I was a failure. I felt responsible for the stability of my family, and as strange as this seems, I felt compassion for my abuser. I actually felt responsibility for keeping him out of trouble, at least up until this point.

Sometime after the sun had set, I walked into her room sobbing and scared. The television was on just loud enough to be an annoyance to my already scared and confused demeanor. She was lying on the right side of the king-size bed that was facing the door as you walked in. She had her gold-rimmed bifocals resting on the tip of her nose as she read the newspaper. On her left sat a large pile of clean but unfolded clothes. She had already removed her makeup and sat comfortably propped against the headboard with several pillows cushioning her back. The comforter that covered her legs was unimpressive and dull, to the point that I cannot remember the color of fabric it was made of. Its low thread count was obvious from the clumping of cotton between the thin, wrinkled layers of partial polyester that held the two sides together.

I stood in the doorway staring at her with a thousand thoughts racing through my mind and my tongue frozen to the roof of my mouth. She stopped reading and looked up at me over her glasses. "What's wrong?" she asked.

The tears were already rolling continuously down my cheeks. "There's something I need to tell you."

"What is it, honey?"

How do I say this? What do I say?

"Well, it's about Dad. He ... he did something to me."

"What did he do?"

What did he do? Duh? Isn't that enough? Are you really going to make me tell you? Oh God ... how do I say this?

"Well, what is it?"

"He ... um ... he ... he touched me."

He touched me. You idiot. Is that all you can say?

"What do you mean touched you? Touched you where?"

Are you kidding me? Am I really going to have to say it?

"Down there," I muttered.

Please don't make me say anything else. I can't. Please just hold me. Please tell me it will be okay, and you'll fix it, and he won't ever do it to me again. Please. I need you to hold me.

"Go to your room."

"But …"

"I said, go to your room." She removed the glasses as tears welled up in her eyes. She was visibly upset.

Oh no. I've hurt her. I didn't mean to hurt her. I just wanted her to fix it. I shouldn't have told her. I should have protected her.

"Are you okay?" I couldn't stand to see her crying. I was standing there feeling more compassion for her than she could feel for me.

"Just go to your room, and stay in there until I come get you."

I walked halfway down the hall and heard her pick up the phone and call my father at work. I stood at the doorway to listen.

"You need to come home *now*. I think you know what it's about."

She hung up the phone, and I hurried to my bedroom. I sat on my bed for what seemed like forever. I just sat there alone and I cried. I thought about all the things that could be about to happen. I listened for the police to knock on the door, and I figured someone would be coming to take me away. I was wrong.

A couple of hours later my parents walked into my room together. He was crying and upset. She was not. My father sat down on my vanity bench, and my mother sat on my bed. He was wearing the same red shorts he'd had on earlier in the day, this time accompanied by a T-shirt. He seemed genuinely upset, but considering the circumstances, there was no sense of desperation or guilt on his face. He looked "caught."

"Go sit on your father's knee," my mother demanded. "He has something he'd like to say."

Sit on his knee? Are you serious?

I remember my vanity was placed to the left of the doorway, and he turned the bench that normally faced the vanity mirror around to face the opposite way. I sat on his left knee, and he placed his left hand in the small of my back. I can remember cringing and curling my back in disgust.

My mother was sitting directly in front of us, with her hands folded in front of her. She showed little emotion besides a determined look that she often got on her face. She was intent on fixing the situation, on keeping me quiet.

"Amanda, I want you to know that I would never do anything to hurt you. Like I explained to your mother, I was only trying to teach you what to do if someone else tried to mess with you. It wasn't what it seemed."

What? I couldn't believe what I was hearing.

"But …"

"Just listen to him," my mother interrupted. "He's very sorry."

"This isn't at all what it seems to be. Your mom and I could get into a lot of trouble if you ever tell anybody about this. Do you understand?"

Then why would you do it? I can't believe this.

I just nodded.

I can't believe this is actually happening. She didn't even ask me.

"If you tell people about this, they won't understand, and we will get into trouble. I wasn't trying to hurt you. I was trying to teach you. That's all. It won't ever happen again."

Teach me? What's that suppose to mean?

I felt molested for the first time all over again. I felt a sense of betrayal far deeper than what I had already experienced. My mother's response was such a devastating blow. This day was another day that would change who I was forever. I remember sitting in the corner of my closet, curled in a fetal position, rocking back and forth, for what seemed like hours. I had finally told. But nobody came to save me.

I wanted to believe that my father was truly sorry, but I knew better. My mother wouldn't listen to me. She minimized his abuse. They made me feel like I was the bad person for misinterpreting his behavior. My mother never asked me any questions. She never asked me exactly what had happened or for how long. She went to him for the answers.

The very next day when my mother left for work, he tried again. I was determined that he wasn't going to take advantage of me anymore. I ignored his calls, and he didn't force me to come. Several days later he tried again. I once again ignored him. He came out of the bedroom, but I was prepared. I ran for the front door and screamed at him.

"You're not going to do this to me anymore. I'll tell. I swear to God, I will run out of this door and tell the first person I see."

There really wasn't any part of my threat that was true. I knew that if my own mother didn't believe me, nobody else would either. I'm not sure where that courage had come from. I would say anything to get him to stop. I couldn't stand to live like that anymore. If he wouldn't stop, I was going to kill myself. I just couldn't stand to live another day. I thought the only way I could end my suffering would be to end my life.

He tried a few more times after that, but never pushed me. He would never molest me again, but I would spend the next twelve years trying to get my mother to believe me.

Chapter 6

Coping with the Silence

ϒ

I've always had this ability to separate myself from the abuse. As I mentioned before, I often would think of myself as two different people: the conventional me, and then the abused. The second persona was the victim, and she developed almost immediately after the first time my father molested me. Children are very resilient by nature, and I am quite certain that the extent of the damage I experienced would not have been nearly as severe if I had gotten help sooner.

If my mother had listened to me—if she had taken me away from my abuser and searched out the help I needed—even after four years of sexual abuse, I now believe that there would have been fewer open sores in my psyche, and those that I did have would have healed more easily. Keeping the secret was the destructive force that was pulling me under.

My father had spent a great deal of time carefully manipulating and grooming me for the abuse. Looking back, he probably groomed me for a year before he ever acted. Grooming is the term used to describe the way sexual predators will slowly isolate their victims, place them in uncomfortable situations, and fill their minds with hopelessness. By the time the actual abuse occurs, the victims are left feeling somewhat responsible because they aren't sure at what point the line was actually crossed.

Intellectually, I understood, even from very early on, that I could not control the abuse that was occurring. My father had complete power over my mind, my body, and my soul. The moment that he first molested me, a part of me died, as if he had amputated a piece of my soul that I could never get back.

Even to this day, I feel that pain. This type of abuse doesn't just change how you think, act, and believe. The very essence of who you are, down to the deepest core, is changed forever. And no matter how much you heal, the person you were before the abuse began will remain irretrievably lost.

I had started my therapy in January, and now it was May. By this point, I had managed to share with Diana in great detail the abuse I had suffered. I was brutally honest with her. As our weekly sessions continued, I began to make major progress. I no longer felt like the victim. I was a survivor. I started to realize that I could choose not to live in the bubble, but escaping wouldn't be easy. My therapy with Diana helped me to understand the choices I had made as a child, the choices that helped me to survive.

"Why do you think you didn't attempt to tell anyone after you first told your mom?" Diana asked.

She had asked me this question several times before, but my answer had always been that I didn't think I would be believed. Now I understood that my silence went much deeper than that.

"I just felt so much responsibility for my family."

"What does that mean?" Diana prodded.

"Well, it's like in my mind, I felt like if I told, then I was the one who would break up the family. I still wasn't sure that I was even experiencing enough abuse that anyone would do anything."

This was such a comfortable session. Our conversation was candid, and very therapeutic. Diana and I maintained our usual positions; I was sitting on the far left side of the couch, and she was directly in front of me in her chair, sitting with her left leg crossed over her right.

"So the lines between normal and abnormal were still entangled?"

"Yeah. I mean … I don't even think I had enough vocabulary to tell what was happening to me. I didn't even know what the word 'molest' meant, so I didn't really know that's what he was doing to me. Does that even make sense?"

"Of course it does," she said. "What did you tell yourself about what was happening?"

"I would try to think of all the things in my mind that were worse than the abuse I was suffering and just be thankful that those things weren't happening."

"So… you minimized it."

"Oh yeah. Big time. I had convinced myself that other people had suffered from abuse worse than I had and that to feel sorry for myself was somehow nonproductive."

The only way that I could deal with the gravity of the abuse was to minimize it to myself. Instead of focusing on the abuse that was occurring, I continued to lock away my memories, as best I could, in my box marked "the abused."

"And do you realize that minimization is a normal coping mechanism. You told yourself whatever you had to just to survive."

"I do. I realize that now."

Even when I talk to survivors today, many times they will minimize their own abuse. They will say, "What you experienced was so much worse." But that isn't true at all. Many survivors feel the same way whether the abuse happens just once or goes on for years like mine did. This is just one way for our minds to try and cope with the abuse, minimization.

"Tell me some other things you did to survive."

"I don't know … what do you mean *survive?*"

"As a child, you had to find ways to survive your situation on a daily basis. Tell me something you did to help your mind escape."

"Well, you're probably gonna think I'm crazy, but there are several years that I honestly can't really remember. It's like they're just a blur."

"That is very common among sexual abuse victims," Diana explained. "It doesn't mean you're crazy. In fact, it is a very normal and healthy response to an abnormal situation. Remember when we talked before about normal reactions to abnormal situations?"

"Yes."

"When people are put in extremely traumatizing situations, the mind has an amazing capability to detach itself. Your mind detached itself so many times that you have lapses of time in your memory. That numbing helped you to survive. Make sense?"

"Yeah … that makes a lot of sense."

I can distinctly remember events in my life that were life-altering, soul-changing experiences. I can still remember sometimes how things smelled, vivid colors that were present, noises that were insignificant, and details that seem ordinary. But there are several years of abuse that are very blurred. These are the years that I numbed myself, purposely detached my mind in order to lose time.

"Now think back to some of the times you can remember. Tell me what you did to survive."

I told her how I used to fantasize about running away, only my fantasy was childlike, completely oblivious to reality. I would think of ways I could construct a house in the deep woods at the back of the fifty acres. I could eat from the fruit trees in the summertime and eat nuts in the winter. I would live all by myself, even if only until I ran out of food. In my mind, this was very realistic.

I even packed a sack full of clothes several times just trying to live out my fantasy. I would take my sack of clothes down to the woods all the way to the creek and spend hours or even most of the day down there. I felt so peaceful. I could hear all the beautiful sounds of nature. When I was alone and hiding, I felt that nobody knew I existed. There was me, nature, and God, and nobody could hurt me.

The birds would sing, and the creek flowed just fast enough to make a slight trickle. The wind would sound loud in all the trees and then die down again, and the leaves would crackle under my feet as I walked.

The grounds were covered in hundreds of Indian paintbrushes, like a pallet of color amid all the weeds. They were my favorite. I loved their bittersweet smell and the way they waved freely in the wind. I wanted to be just like them, full of vigor and free.

I also fantasized about the day I could leave. I knew that I would have to do well in school in order to have a way out. I needed a scholarship, so I continued to focus on my schoolwork. I made good grades and even finished a few college classes before I graduated from high school.

You found such positive ways to cope," Diana said. "Can't you see how resilient you are?"

"In some ways I can. But then everything I accomplished seemed to further fuel the image our family had. People would tell me how lucky I was to have such a great family, that obviously my parents had raised me well, and how people would love to have parents like I had. It just burned me. I had so much anger built up inside and nowhere to vent it."

"I'm sure you did. But what was the alternative?"

"Drugs and alcohol," I said, chuckling.

"Right. And you never turned to them."

"Never."

"That's amazing."

"I guess. It just wasn't ever an option. I knew that my only real way out was to make a better life for myself."

"It just amazes me that you thought like that at such a young age. Statistically, your success in life is a miracle."

"I know. I'm very lucky."

"Maybe 'lucky' isn't the right word. How about perseverant?"

"You're right. Much better." We were both laughing this time.

Our session came to an end soon thereafter, and I was to come back again the following week.

§

In high school, I was incredibly shy. I was a member of International Baccalaureate (IB), which is a college preparatory program. I was the kid who always chose the back corner seat of the class and had my homework every day ready to turn in. Sure, there were days that I finished assignments during lunch, but I always had my homework ready when due.

As a teenager, my parents really had me convinced that I must be crazy. I started to question my own memory, my own feelings, and everything that I considered to be factual. I even questioned my spirituality. I thought, *How could God the Father love me and care for me and protect me if my earthly father failed at his duty?* I didn't understand how I could ever trust a God who was referred to as male.

Through all my experience of locking away my abuse in my box, the spiritual abuse would not stay there. Christianity had always played a big role in my life, and even throughout the abuse I continued to be active in my church. I was a leader in my youth group. In many ways, this helped me escape the abuses I was experiencing because I had a place to go that I felt was safe. But in return I was even more confused by the spiritual abuse, because being in church was a constant reminder of the drastic difference I faced every time I had to go home.

I was fortunate to have an amazing youth minister who I really looked up to as a father figure. Phillip wasn't a typical clean-cut young Baptist youth minister. He was approaching fifty years old, with gray hair and a nicely trimmed gray beard. His appearance came across as rather scraggly if you didn't know him, but his heart was genuine, and he took his calling seriously.

There were several times I tried to tell Phillip about my abuse. Like the time I was twelve and our youth group took a weekend trip to Dallas. We were there for a two-day youth conference that included one Friday night session and one Saturday morning session where several popular Christian music artists would perform and an evangelistic preacher would deliver messages important in a teenager's life. We were joined by over 20,000 other teenagers at Reunion Arena.

We returned to our hotel Friday night well after midnight, and only after stopping off for a quick bite at Taco Bell. Phillip and I were sitting side by side on the stairs outside talking. I had been best friends with his daughter for several years, so he had really developed a major influence in my life.

We'd been talking for at least fifteen minutes when I finally got enough nerve to say:

"I just feel really upset all the time."

There was no way he could have guessed what I was really trying to tell him. I'm sure he must have thought our conversation was pointless, and that sleep was way more important, but he sat on the step patiently letting me hint my way through my problems.

"Why?" he asked.

"I don't know … I just … I can't get along with my brother," I blurted out. My words didn't even make sense to me. *Can't get along with my brother? You idiot. What are you talking about?*

"Most people your age can't get along well with their siblings. That's normal. It'll get better as you grow older."

"No, I know. I mean … It's not just that. I …" *Say it. Just tell him you don't want to go home.* "I just feel like sometimes I don't even want to go home." *Oh God. What have I said? Cover it up. Just think of something. Quick.*

"Why would you …?"

"I just mean that I wish we didn't fight so much, and it's seems easier being at church around all my friends." *You're such an idiot. You don't even make any sense. He's gonna think you're an idiot.*

"I can understand that," he said.

I could tell he was trying his best to sympathize, and he remained patient with me the entire time. But I quickly ended the conversation. I wanted to tell him, but I felt like he was too well accustomed to the bubble. He was too close to me. I know that doesn't make a lot of sense, but he knew my family too well.

Phillip is probably the reason that I stayed active in church for as long as I did. I needed his influence and guidance in my life. But deep down, I really felt as though God had deserted me when I needed him the most. My church taught me that purity was sacred, and my father stole that from me. He stole from me the right to explore sexuality for myself. He used the Bible to justify himself. He twisted God's word to make himself feel okay about his behavior with no regard to the effect his words were having on me.

My father not only abused me mentally, physically, emotionally and sexually, he committed abuse that is rarely, if ever, identified or acknowledged: spiritual abuse. To abuse a person with a spiritual element is to not only have zero regard for their physical being, but ultimately no concern for their soul. This abuse is as profound as any other category of abuse and perhaps the most difficult to overcome.

Chapter 7

Confrontations

ɤ

The year after I first told my mother about Dad's abusive behavior, I was even more suicidal than before. I was just fifteen years old, but the secret was killing me. I felt like the weight of a thousand bricks was sitting on my chest twenty-four hours a day. Nonstop pressure. Nonstop anxiety. The replay of events again and again in my head was making me feel crazy.

Each day in my parents' home had become more torturous than the last. Every day I thought of killing myself or running away or pondered who I would tell. I would fantasize about living with other people that I knew. Putting myself somewhere else—*anywhere*—was my first thought in the morning and my last before falling asleep.

I began writing about the things my father had done to me. I was brutally honest. I cussed at him in my writings, and every page was filled with anger and hatred. Then, not long after I started to keep my journal, my newly discovered escape mechanism was extinguished. Literally.

One evening, after school, my parents called me into the living room. My brother was at work, and the sun had already set. In my mother's hand was the cheap spiral notebook that contained all my deepest thoughts.

"We need to talk."

The blood immediately rushed to my head, and I felt like my cheeks were burning red with shame.

"Your mom found this in your room today while she was cleaning," my father said.

Cleaning? Yeah, right. Don't you mean snooping?

"You can't write things like this!" my mom exclaimed. "Do you have any idea how much trouble we could be in if someone was to find you had written something like this? You just can't be doing this."

Why do you always make me feel bad for wanting to tell? Do you have any idea what this secret is doing to me? Do you?

I couldn't speak. My body was numb again. I was rigid with silence.

"We have decided it will be best to burn this journal, just get rid of it completely. We don't want to ever find anything like this again. Do you understand?" My mom showed no emotion about the words she had read. There was only disgust and anger for me. I was the problem, clearly. I just nodded my head.

They were well prepared, with the charcoal grill on the back patio already lit and the vertical blinds covering the glass door pushed to the far left. I watched my mother walk to the sliding glass door, open it, and walk over to the grill without hesitation. She was ripping out the pages where I'd written my heart out in an attempt to save myself. She threw all of my words on the fire, walked back inside, and handed me the remains of my spiral.

"Go to your room," she commanded.

She was so cold. I was standing there traumatized by what had just happened. She felt no need to hug me, no need to comfort me. Her only concern was how she was going to continue to shut me up. I walked back to my room and cried myself to sleep.

§

I was sixteen the next time I attempted to tell my mother. By this time, my relationship with her had drastically deteriorated. We constantly fought. I was angry at her all the time because I felt she had betrayed me.

I started working as a cashier at the local grocery store as soon as I turned sixteen, and we shared a car for a while. She was driving me to work one day when another argument began. We continued our petty disagreement until she called me a liar, and the subject quickly changed.

"You're the one who's a liar," I blurted out. *How can I be the bad one? I'm not the one with the attitude. I hate myself. I hate my life. You don't even love me.*

"What have I lied about?" she asked.

"What *haven't* you lied about? You never believe anything I say." There was a part of me that just hated her. I despised her because she treated me like a disease.

"What are you talking about?"

"You know what I'm talking about. How could you have not believed me?" *What am I talking about? You're unbelievable. Uugggh … I can't stand you.*

"Amanda, you're going to have to refresh my memory because I don't have a clue what you're talking about."

Of course you don't because you get to live your life every day without thinking about it, but I think about it every day, all day.

"How could you not remember? You know exactly what I'm talking about. About what Dad did to me?"

"You admitted you had exaggerated that."

What? Either you're crazy, or I am.

"Exaggerated? When did I ever say I had exaggerated that?"

Here we go. I can't believe you're going to do this to me.

"You admitted that you had lied about it, to get attention."

"Are you kidding me? Are you serious? You actually believe that? I never said I had lied about it. You and Dad are the ones who said it didn't happen. You told me that it wasn't what I thought it was. I know exactly what it was. He molested me. Not just once. Over and over and over."

"This is the first I am hearing about this."

"The first you're hearing of it? You wouldn't let me tell you. You wouldn't let me speak."

"I'm not going to talk about this with you right now, Amanda."

"When *are* you going to talk about it?"

"This conversation is over. You admitted that you made it all up for attention. You have always done that. You've always been a liar."

I want to puke. I want to jump out of this car while it is rolling. Please, God, just kill me. Take me out of this misery. I remember in that moment feeling defeated, like she was trying to make me crazy. I couldn't understand where in the world she was coming from. But I was certain she had convinced herself of her own lies.

When we arrived at my work, I exited the car, slammed the door, and headed toward the store, still crying. I walked in while trying to tie my apron and wiping the tears from my face. Five minutes later, I was smiling at the customers, asking them about their day, and listening to their complaints about every minor detail of our business.

§

Life continued as usual. I was working full time, but still managed to maintain my grades. I stayed in my honors classes because I knew I needed a scholarship in order to go to college. I knew I had to plan for my future. I'm still not sure how I knew that, but I was desperate for something different. I dreamed of being a different person.

The stress of maintaining grades in the IB program, along with working a full-time job, in addition to everything that was going on at home, was giving me stomach ulcers. The doctors were baffled. They didn't know why a teenager would have so many stomach problems.

The pressure I felt to uphold our family image was just too much. I drifted away from all my friends, including our youth minister's daughter, and eventually I stopped going to church. Not having friends just seemed easier than pretending I was someone else. I figured that they didn't really know me anyway, and if they did, they probably wouldn't want to be my friends. There were very few people with whom I felt comfortable, and I avoided most social situations in which I would have to interact closely with others.

§

Another year passed, and I met my future husband, Daniel. We have the silliest love story. I was seventeen, and he was eighteen. I was still working as a cashier, and Daniel got a job at our grocery store as a sacker. Trivial as this may sound now, winning "Sacker of the Year" was quite an honor as a teenager, especially since the title came along with a raise. He was to be honored at the annual company dinner and asked me to come along as his date.

What girl could resist a young, muscular man with dark hair and dimples? We instantly felt a deep connection for one another, and the friendship we shared was unique for two lovers at such a young age.

We'd been dating for less than a year when I began to drop hints of my sketchy past.

"You just don't know my dad," I'd always say. "He's so different than he acts around other people."

One of the best days of my life came when my father awoke without realizing Daniel was in the house. My father stormed down the hallway, raging at everything he saw that was out of order, and lost control as he reached the kitchen because there were a few dirty dishes in the sink. Daniel and I were sitting in my bedroom with the door closed.

"What's wrong with him?" Daniel asked me.

"What do you mean?"

"Why is he so mad?"

"I don't know. He's always like this when he wakes up. He'll get mad for no reason. He'll say that something stinks or the house is a wreck and just get mad."

A distinct crashing sound began to echo throughout the house.

"Is he breaking the plates?" Daniel asked. He nudged my bedroom door open just enough to catch a glimpse of my father taking one plate after another and slamming them into the countertop hard enough for them to shatter.

"I'm so sorry you have to see this." I was embarrassed.

"Amanda, get in here now," my father yelled.

I was afraid of how Daniel would react. He had never experienced such absurdness before. His parents had always treated him with dignity and respect and had demonstrated nothing but love and self-control.

"Let me go first," Daniel insisted.

Before I could object, he had already stepped into the hallway ahead of me. My father stood dumbfounded in Daniel's presence. His demeanor changed from hostility and rage to extreme calm in only a matter of seconds. The feeling in the room became very awkward.

"Hey, Daniel," my father stuttered.

Daniel looked into my father's eyes with complete disgust.

"Hey," he replied, trying desperately to remain cordial after losing all respect for the man who stood in front of him.

"I didn't know you were here," my father said, still struggling to gain his composure.

Nothing else was said as Daniel and I made our way back into my bedroom. My father cleaned up all the broken pieces of glass and tried hard to pretend as though his immaturity had not been witnessed.

"I get it," Daniel said, looking straight into my eyes as the tears welled up and began falling down my cheeks. "I understand what you mean now. How you always say he is different than he seems. I get it."

The strange thing is that my father's behavior that day was incredibly normal and nothing out of the ordinary for me. But Daniel was able to catch a glimpse of a person who was behaving very differently than he let on to outsiders. That's why I felt like that day was one of the best days of my life. Until that point, nobody else had seen that side of my father, and now my secret life was being revealed to someone who had a much clearer perspective than I did.

I started spending all my spare time with Daniel. He and I were best friends and shared all our deepest thoughts and secrets with one another. Besides my mother, he is the first person I ever told about my abuse. We were only kids: I had just turned eighteen, and he had not yet had his nineteenth birthday.

I can't even remember why I decided to tell him, other than the fact that I felt I was keeping secrets from him that would keep him from getting to know who I truly was. I wasn't exactly forthcoming when I did tell him, still apprehensive from all the rejection I'd received from my mother.

I remember saying "My dad did things to me that he shouldn't have done." I begged Daniel not to tell anyone. I didn't tell him any details at the time and never mentioned my failed attempts to tell my mother. I remember him being angry at my father but feeling as though he had no way to vent. I made him promise not to say anything. He held me as I cried and gave me his word.

We were still children, trying our best to cope with adult issues, with brains that were not developed enough to do so. But he never once doubted me, and never pushed for more information. He allowed me to divulge as much or as little as I needed to and at whatever time I felt I could.

§

I graduated from high school on June 3, 2000. High school graduation didn't prove to be much of a big deal for me. I knew that my education wasn't complete, and furthermore, I knew that I would be independent soon after. My parents had always told us that we could stay until we graduated high school, and then we were to move out on our own. They would allow us to move into the trailer, broken down as it might be, to help with the transition. Then shortly after, we were to become completely independent. David had done just that, and I knew that I would be doing the same.

I moved into the trailer the week I graduated. Even though I didn't have a choice about moving out, I definitely didn't put up a fight. I probably would rather have been homeless than have to live in my parents' house for one more day.

I got a presidential scholarship to Tyler Junior College and started working toward my degree in dental hygiene. I continued to work at the grocery store and spent my first year of college just trying to adapt to the adult world I had been dumped into.

I was still seeing my parents often back then because I was living directly behind them. But living in the trailer became psychologically difficult for me. I had only lived there a few months when the nightmares and flashback became overwhelming. I was reliving many years of abuse that I had attempted to swallow for all these years. The abuse had occurred in both homes but had started in the trailer. My bedroom was now the very room where all the abuse had first begun.

Reliving my abuse made me miss the comfort I had once felt in the church. Daniel had been raised in the Assembly of God church, and I was raised Southern Baptist. We'd been dating for two years, and neither of us had attended church since we started dating, but religion had played an important role in both of our lives. So Daniel and I started attending a contemporary Baptist church together.

At first, I enjoyed going back to church, but I didn't realize how confused I was spiritually. The confusion I felt was amplified with every sermon, and my presence in church became another psychological amplifier to me. I didn't understand anything back then. I knew that I was a nervous wreck, but I had no perception as to why. I just thought I was crazy.

Our pastor was also a licensed psychologist. I met with him a few times, but the therapy was too much for my young mind. I wasn't ready to talk about my childhood yet. I backed away from church again, unable to cope with the immense strain I felt from my past, and focused on my schoolwork. I was unable to sleep, often turning on all the lights in the trailer and lying on the couch until the sun came up.

This is the point at which I began controlling my life with food. Many people cannot understand this concept, but eating disorders oftentimes have little to do with weight. I felt like my entire life was out of control, and the only thing I had power over was food. I could control how much or how little I consumed, and I could exercise to change my body. I wanted to look and feel like a different person. I punished myself by withholding food. My goal was to eat less than eight hundred calories a day and exercise away most of that eight hundred. I felt I didn't deserve to eat, because I didn't deserve to be alive.

Unfortunately, when this type of mind-set begins, there is an incredible payoff. Watching the changes in your body and stepping on the scale become intoxicating. I remember exercising for hours trying to burn off the calories I had eaten that day. I would often burn over a thousand calories in one exercise session. I was mostly successful with my daily calorie goal, many times eating only half that much. I felt addicted to the adrenaline my body would release from those workouts. This type of control became my new coping mechanism.

I knew that I needed to find a way out of the trailer and move somewhere more psychologically safe. So my second year of college, I moved into a garage apartment located just a few miles from the college and just around the corner from the grocery store where I still worked.

§

I had become increasingly visibly depressed, shaking constantly, losing weight, and slipping further away every day.

There were several items of mine I had left behind in the trailer that my mother had boxed up and set aside for me in the house. When I went to her house to pick them up, the changes in my body had become more apparent than ever, and my increasing hostility was easier to set off in her presence.

"Are you okay?" she asked me. "You haven't seemed yourself lately."

"No. I'm not okay. I'm depressed. I am having a really hard time right now."

"Why? Is it school?"

"No, it isn't school. School is going fine. I'm just depressed. You won't understand."

"You can tell me."

Yeah right. I can tell you if I want to fight with you.

"I can't talk to you about it," I said. "You'll just get mad."

"No, I won't. Talk to me."

"I can't stop thinking about what happened to me."

My abuse was the foremost thing on my mind. I couldn't understand how everyone else wasn't always thinking about the abuse too.

"What are you talking about? What happened?"

She tried to seem concerned, but I knew our conversation was quickly going downhill.

"Well, you know what happened. I know that you don't believe me about what Dad did to me, but I don't need you to believe me anymore. I don't need you to accept that it happened, because I know it did."

I really wanted to believe what I was saying, but I didn't. I really needed her to grab me and cry for me. I needed her to accept and validate my feelings, even though she had shut me out so many times before. She put her head down and started to cry.

"Are you going to prosecute him?"

Prosecute him? You're more concerned about him than you are me.

"Am *I* going to? Shouldn't you have been the one to do that?"

"I don't know."

"I can't believe you would ask me that. Of all the things you could say, you are concerned about whether or not I am going to prosecute him?"

"Well, what do you want me to do?" Her tone became hostile.

"I want you to be my mother and believe me. I want you to support me."

"I just don't know what to believe."

Why don't you just sit here and call me a liar again? You know what to believe, you just don't know what you want to believe.

I was angry. This was the first time that she had even acknowledged my abuse, yet she cried for her husband, and felt little, if any compassion for me. I left abruptly and spent the evening brooding over our conversation.

People were still under the impression that everything was blissful in my family. I had a hard time surviving on my own. I was beyond poor. But being poor and struggling was still better than having to go back home. Dental hygiene school was rigorous and took all my spare time. My whole life was out of control. Both my parents were patients for me while I was in school. We continued to play the game. The bubble was sturdy, and nothing could penetrate the barrier.

Daniel was in college too but still lived at home with his parents. As much as he tried to understand my struggles, I had been forced to hold much more responsibility in my life than he could have possibly related to. Though our limited time together certainly strained our relationship at moments, Daniel remained the one constant in my life.

Our relationship had grown to the point that we knew we would one day be married. I was starting to become very close to his parents as well. They were beginning to see past my parents' facade by listening to the inconsistencies in their stories.

"Things just don't add up," Daniel's mom would say. "Your parents just don't seem to be who they say they are." She would never elaborate back then, and I sure wasn't going to add any details to her suspicion.

His parents were always such genuine, kind, and sincere people. They were easy to love. They made sure I had groceries to eat, and often slipped me hundred-dollar bills to help me with my rent.

§

I graduated magna cum laude from dental hygiene school in May of 2003. On June 21, only a month later, I married my high school sweetheart, Daniel. By then, my brother David and I had managed to share many details of our abuse with each other, but I had never discussed the sexual abuse with him. As far as I knew, David still wasn't aware any sexual abuse had occurred.

David was well aware of my feelings toward my father though, and he knew how desperately I wanted him, not my father, to walk me down the aisle. I felt trapped, because everyone assumed we were the perfect family and that I was Daddy's little girl. The questions that would come if my father didn't walk me down the aisle were questions I was nowhere near ready to answer.

That turned out to be one of those moments in my life that I truly regret. I wish I had been at a place in my life where my wedding was about me and what I wanted, and not about how our family appeared to the outside world.

My father had been ill for many years with his epilepsy. I secretly wished that he would feel too sick to walk me down the aisle. But he felt fine. I remember walking down the aisle in my beautiful white gown, with my arm enlaced in my father's. I was looking around at all the people, but I was smiling through my anger. I thought about how foolish our act seemed to be, and about all the people who were being tricked by our facade. In that moment, I felt responsible. I was becoming just like my parents.

In the receiving line at our wedding, a woman leaned over to Daniel and said, "She was Daddy's little girl before she was yours."

When she walked away, Daniel leaned into me, patted me on the back, and said, "If she only knew."

I was excited about the commitment that I was making to my husband before God, but the actual wedding event seemed like another fake part of my very fake life.

After I married Daniel, I was able to pull myself out of my unhealthy relationship with food and my addiction to exercise. I still am not sure about when I stopped or why, but at some point, God saved me from that. Don't underestimate the miracle that took place. I didn't even realize I had an eating disorder until Diana explained to me why I had developed those habits as a coping mechanism. So my healing was definitely a miracle. I struggled off and on for several years, and I never had any formal treatment for my eating disorder, but I still managed to overcome the feelings of control that the disorder gave me.

Chapter 8

Validation

γ

In the spring of 2004 my anger had become uncontainable. Daniel had begun working in law enforcement as a local city policeman just a few months before we got married. Experience in law enforcement made maintaining composure around my father difficult for Daniel, and he began to express concern for any relationship my mother and father might have with our future children. His concerns made me start thinking too. I didn't feel like I could have a child as long as my relationship with my parents had not been addressed and properly dealt with.

Sitting on the couch at my parent's house one day, I was watching the news as another story of child abuse made the headlines. I kept thinking, *At least they escaped. At least they were found, and they have a chance.* But as I sat there, grateful for the rescue those children had been lucky to receive, my father had the audacity to comment about how wrong the parents were for treating their children in that way.

I was infuriated. I didn't understand who this man was, what his thought process was, and how he could live with himself, knowing what he had done. Did he think I didn't remember? I just couldn't believe he could make a comment like that and actually look in the mirror every morning, feeling peace about the life he had led.

I left their house abruptly, not bothering to hide how disturbed I was, and drove home, crying all the way there. Every day that I was living in this lie was another day that I was not living at all. I logged on to my computer and began arguing with my mother through IM about his comments, and she came to his defense once again. She didn't want to talk about the specifics of my abuse, but I continued to egg her on.

My brother called me in the midst of our argument, and I began venting my anger toward her. I was beyond frustration. Until that point, David and I had mostly joked about our abuse. We talked a lot about the similarity of our memories, but in more of a humorous fashion. I know this seems strange, but we had an odd way of making jokes out of what we went through. We understood each other, but we still had never talked about the sexual abuse.

"There are things that you just don't know about, David. Things that happened. Terrible things."

"I do know," he said.

"No you don't, David. If you knew everything that they did to me, you would understand where I am coming from."

"Mandy, I do know."

"No you don't. You don't understand. He molested me, David. And I think he even tried to kill me once. I told her, and she didn't do anything. She didn't believe me. She still doesn't believe me."

At that point, my brother revealed to me that he, too, often felt fearful for our lives. He would sometimes take the ammunition out of my father's guns and hide the bullets under his mattress while we were sleeping. He was afraid my father would kill us in our sleep.

"Tell her that she needs to talk to me." David was on the phone with me while I was typing back and forth with my mother. "Tell her that I know, and she needs to talk to me."

"She says that she doesn't want to talk to you about this because it is between us."

"No. She needs to talk to me."

"Why? What are you gonna say?"

"Mandy, I know what happened to you. I've known for a long time."

"I don't understand."

"I knew he was messing with you, and I placed a tape recorder in the bedroom," he revealed. "I caught it on tape. I heard it."

"Oh my God."

A tape? Oh, thank God! Finally! Finally, now she will believe me. Wow. A tape. Thank God!

I was crying hysterically, and I could hear my brother crying too.

I was amazed. I couldn't believe that he'd had the courage to do such a thing, and I immediately felt validated. I felt like all the doubts my parents tried to instill in me were gone, and I finally knew that I had someone on my side. Both my parents had tried to program me, but my mother tried to shut me up. She wanted me to believe that I was crazy, and that I was terrible for even accusing my father of doing such a horrific thing.

"Please … please call her. Please tell her about the tape. Do you still have it?" I knew he was the only one she would listen to. I felt that, if she heard it from him, she would at least take notice.

"I don't know if I do or not. I'm not sure what happened to it. It doesn't matter because I know what was on it."

"Don't tell me. I don't want to know. I can't know."

"It's okay. I'm going to call her now, and I will call you back."

"Okay. Thank you. Thank you so much."

He told her she needed to believe me, and he told her about the tape, but I don't think she let him get much else in. She then believed that maybe something had happened, but she still wasn't sure what. She told him that she couldn't handle the pressure and that she never wanted to talk about any abuse again. She refused to speak to me about the tape or the abuse. She wanted me to "get over it."

Telling a survivor to just get over his or her abuse is, in my opinion, the most insensitive comment a person can possibly make. That approach is no different than telling a person with cancer to just wish themselves well and quit complaining about the pain. When something happens in your life that changes who you are as a person, the experience becomes a part of you, and to "just get over it" would mean forgetting about a significant part of who you have become, which would be impossible.

§

A couple of days passed and I began to feel an intense urge to confront my father. I was sick of always looking to my mother for answers and hearing her defend him. I wanted to hear him answer for himself. I had so many questions to ask him, and I wanted to hear him admit to me what he had done.

My mother refused to be present because she "just couldn't handle it." She knew I was going to confront him, but she said this issue was between my father and me. I think she just didn't want to hear him admit what he had done.

I finally built up enough courage to go the following week. The thoughts of his reaction were harrowing, to say the least. I started to think of all the ways I could get away if he tried to hurt me. I mapped out escape routes from his home and even convinced myself I could run faster than he could, if I needed to get away. On one level, I thought that what I was doing was crazy, but on another, I knew the confrontation was necessary.

Daniel didn't want me to go. Not because he thought the confrontation wasn't necessary, but because he was afraid for my safety. I insisted on going alone.

"I just don't trust him," Daniel told me.

"This is something I have to do," I explained. "I just need to know you'll support me. I know you're worried, but I have to do this."

"Of course I'll support you. I just don't think it's a good idea for you to go alone."

I knew he was right, but I went alone anyway. I kept thinking that I had to shield Daniel from the entire truth. I thought that if Daniel knew exactly what all my father had done to me, he would lose affection for me.

My heart was pounding so fast that I could literally feel my entire body shake with every beat. *What will I say? How will I say it?*

I pulled up to his house, and he was standing in the driveway. My mother must have warned him that I would be coming, because he knew exactly why I was there.

"Do you want to talk?" he asked.

"Don't you think we should? If you know what's best for you, you'll talk about it."

"Come inside and sit down." He walked in first, and I followed behind. He looked like he usually does with his cheap cotton shorts and plain T-shirt. He was walking with a slight limp, holding a cane in his right hand, the result of a hip replacement that had never fully healed. He was only in his late forties, but his limp, along with his pessimistic attitude, made him appear at least ten years older.

He took a seat in his recliner, and I pulled the piano bench out and sat down, facing him.

"I want to know why," I demanded.

"Why *what?*"

"I want to know why you did this to me. What possessed you to think it was okay to molest your own daughter?"

He hung his head down and mumbled, "I always knew this would come back to haunt me."

"What's that supposed to mean? How about 'I'm sorry,' or 'Please forgive me'? Is that all you can say? You knew it would come back to haunt you?"

The moment was one I will never forget. He crumbled under the pressure and fell to the floor on his knees.

"What do you want me to say?" he cried.

"I want to see that you are sorry. I want to know why you did it. I just don't understand."

"I really don't know why. I have thought about this every single day, and I've wondered if you would ever ask me about it. I just haven't been able to stop thinking about it."

"You've thought about it. You've thought about it? I really don't give a crap what you've had to endure. Do you have any idea what it's done to me?"

"I know I shouldn't have done it."

"Then why did you? Why haven't you ever tried to say you're sorry?"

"I really didn't know how to. I just thought if you didn't bring it up, then neither would I."

"Then why do you always tell Mom you don't remember when she asks you? How could you do this to me, then deny me the memory I know is right?"

"I just didn't want her to know. I thought it would be better to protect her."

"So you can protect her, but not me. That doesn't even make sense."

"I know."

"You're really sick, you know that? You need a lot of help. I don't understand this." As I continued, I became more and more angry. I called him every name in the book. I told him how much his abuse had affected me. He just sat there crying, the same way he had when my mother had confronted him ten years earlier.

"I don't know what to say. I don't know how to make it better," he said.

"You can't make this better. It is what it is, and if you were truly sorry, you would have come to me to apologize. The only reason you are crying now is because I am confronting you."

"I would take it all back if I could."

"Well, I don't know if I believe that. I don't think you're sorry at all. I think you're sorry you got caught. If you felt that bad about it, you wouldn't have kept doing it for all those years. Have you done this to anyone else?"

"No."

"How do I know that? How am I supposed to believe you won't do this to someone else?"

"If I ever thought of doing it again, I would just kill myself."

"Well, you should. You'll never understand what you've done. I don't really know how to move on from this."

I left that day feeling a lot of relief just from having confronted him and hearing him validate what happened, but wondering what I would do next. My mother still didn't want to talk about any aspect of the abuse. She said that she couldn't handle the stress of the past anymore. I was crushed again. Everything she did and thought had only her own interest at heart. She wanted me to forget that the abuse had ever happened. She was determined to silence me.

She emphasized that the past was never to be spoken about again because I had confronted him, and that I needed to forgive him and move forward with my life. But my journey was far from over. In fact, my true healing hadn't even begun. The following January is when my broken spirit would walk into the nurse practitioner's office and check yes beside that little word "depression."

Chapter 9

And the Bubble Bursts

ɤ

I knew that I could never be happy if my molester, my father, continued to be a part of my life. But to break free from him would not be easy, because I would also be breaking free from my secret. People were still under the impression that things were fine in our family. To disown my father would certainly raise a lot of questions that I needed to be prepared to answer. I knew that my mother would present challenges of her own.

I had made strides in my therapy. I had gained so much insight about all the abuse I had suffered, and I had developed self-esteem and self-worth. I had the support of my husband and his parents and finally decided I wasn't going to play the game anymore.

In June of 2005, I decided to end my relationship with my father. I mailed him a hand-written letter telling him good-bye. I explained why I could no longer have a relationship with him, and I told him how much his abuse had affected every aspect of my life. I didn't want to have anger toward him anymore.

Spiritually, I knew I needed to forgive him. But emotionally, up until that point, I couldn't bring myself to give him that absolution. This was partly because I knew that every interaction with him, every conversation for the rest of my life would be faked. I understood that forgiveness was not about him. Instead, the process involved handing back to him what he had done to me and thereby giving up all my feelings of hate toward him.

So I forgave him. Not because I had to, or because that was the right thing to do. No, I forgave him because I wanted to, for me.

I didn't want to carry that baggage around with me any longer. Understanding how to forgive my father took a while for me. I had to learn that forgiving him without then pretending that the abuse had never occurred was okay. I finally came to the point where I knew that I could truly forgive him, even though I never wanted to see him again.

This is what most people never come to understand. *Forgiveness.* The act of forgiving is actually much simpler than we would like to acknowledge. Forgiveness doesn't mean that a person's behavior is either acceptable or forgettable. Forgiving my father meant that I would no longer let what he did to me control my life and my thoughts.

I wanted to be at peace with the letter I would send him—to be able to walk away knowing that I had said everything that I felt was important, but without any responsibility for his reaction to my words.

§

June 6, 2005

I hope you can understand and appreciate the contents of this letter. I have many things I must say to you.

First and foremost, I have truly forgiven you for the horrible things you did to me. I no longer feel anger toward you, nor do I hate you. I understand this issue was confronted last year—all I ask is that you be honest with yourself and read this letter thoroughly.

I know that there is a part of you that truly loves me. I really do know that. But I am unable to comprehend your type of love. The older I get, the more I understand the gravity of what you have done to me. I want you to understand that, although I have truly forgiven you, I cannot and never will forget or be able to pretend as though the abuse never happened. I am still struggling with the effects of the sexual abuse, and mental abuse. You not only sexually abused me; you manipulated me and everyone else in your life. I am still not quite sure who the real you is.

I want you to know that I am very concerned about your salvation. All of the literature I have read strongly suggests that rehabilitating a sexual offender is impossible, and a child molester rarely has just one victim. I often wonder how many victims you've had. You have never attempted to seek professional help for what you did. I must draw the conclusion that, since sexual abuse is a crime of opportunity, given the chance, you will likely abuse again.

I don't believe you felt guilty about what you did because you acted repeatedly and deliberately. You manipulated and confused me. The fact that you could repeatedly molest your daughter with no regard to consequences, and no regard to what effect that abuse would have on me, is completely unfathomable to me. I can't even begin to comprehend how a person's mind can justify that. You stole my innocence. You took my safety. You betrayed my trust and my love. Then you denied what you had done.

Do you realize that my own mother believed you over me? She chose you over me. Made me live in the same house with a man who repeatedly molested me. When I told her, she should have left you. She should have protected me. She should have sent you to prison. She asked me if I was going to prosecute you, but I was a child. A decision like that should never have been left up to me. I guess neither of you will ever understand exactly how horrible and difficult things were for me. She has an unconditional love for you that she never developed for me.

I have finally sought counseling so that I can move on with my life and be normal and healthy. I have realized what an amazingly resilient and awesome person I am to go through everything I endured and still become a normal, intelligent, and moral person. In order for me to remain normal and healthy, I can no longer subject myself to the environment in which I was abused. On the outside, our family pretends as though everything is fine. You pretend as though nothing happened. Dissociating my father from my abuser is impossible for me because they are one and the same.

Being in your house triggers flashbacks and causes me to continue to have Post Traumatic Stress Disorder. I must, and have to, avoid putting my mental health in danger. I can no longer continue a relationship with you that pretends to be normal, because our interaction is just that—pretend. We have not had a normal relationship since I was ten years old. This is not my choice. This was *your* choice.

What I hope for you is that somehow you come to understand your sins and that you are able to respect my feelings. I do not hate you for what you did. I never have hated you, but I do hate your sins. If you come to understand what you've done, you will also respect this letter and appreciate the boundaries I must have to protect myself and my well being.

I was naïve enough to think that he might kill himself when he read my letter. But about a week after I mailed the letter, I received an e-mail from him.

June 14, 2005

I have been thinking the past few days how to respond to your letter. You must first know that I love you very, very much. There is nothing within my grasp that I wouldn't do for either you or David. I believed that when we talked last year it might be possible for us to start healing this old wound. I do however realize it takes time.

I also want you to know that I have an ongoing relationship with the Lord. If I die today, I will go to heaven.

In closing, again, I do love both you and David with all my heart and I will respect your wishes.

Love Dad

Nothing could capture my emotions better than the entry I made in my journal that day:

How do I feel about that letter now that I read it with uncast eyes? It is a letter from a criminal, a child molester. It is not written with human emotion involved. This is a letter from a criminal who knows nothing of his crimes. Remorse cannot exist from someone who enjoyed their acts. What wound does he have? "We" don't have an old wound. "I" have a wound. It is an open, gushing, gaping wound that is just now being treated. My wound has been infected for over ten years. The infection runs through my blood and infects all of me. My heart. My head. My life. There is nothing in his grasp he wouldn't do for me or David? I guess there's nothing he won't do *to* me either. What a sick monster.

§

At that point, I started to realize that he truly was not at all sorry for what he had done—only sorry that he'd been caught. I began to view him as a mentally sick. Of course, there has never been any diagnosis, and I am not a psychologist, but deep down, I thought that's what he was. He had no capability to understand others' feelings, and acted only in what his best interest was in the moment. Looking back, I can still see the anger I had toward him when I wrote that letter, and I would probably write the letter a little differently today. But I don't regret anything I said to him because my thoughts and feelings were an important part of my journey at the time.

I knew that I would eventually hear from my mother. I thought she would be angry, and I just sat waiting for her phone call. A few more weeks passed before that call came. But she didn't mention anything about the letter or recent events. I think she still thought she could ignore everything, and the crisis would go away again. Her denial had reached new proportions.

"Listen, I need you to take your dad to the doctor next week," she said. "I'm going out of town and I don't have anyone to take him."

"Uhhh … No." I was confused.

"Why not?" She acted as though she didn't know.

"Didn't you read the letter I sent to him?"

"Well, yeah, but I need someone to take him to the doctor."

You really are crazy.

"Well, I'm sorry. I can't do it."

"What do you mean you can't do it? I can't believe you won't take your father to the doctor. Who am I supposed to get to take him? Your brother can't take him, and you're the only one. He has to go to his appointment."

"I just can't do it. I don't know what else to say."

She quickly got off the phone, totally oblivious to the seriousness of my situation. She could only perceive things inside the bubble, and seeing me break away was making her angry.

§

I knew that, before long, people would start to ask more questions, but I don't think anything could have prepared me for what was to come.

I was sitting at home late one night the following week when I received a phone call from my Aunt Mindy. Daniel was watching a UFC match in the living room, and I was in the computer room.

Mindy is my father's only sister and my only aunt because my mother does not have siblings. She was completely oblivious to anything that had gone on in our family. She truly thought she had the most wonderful brother who had raised his children with respect and dignity and had no reason to suspect anything other than that.

"Mandy, honey. Honey, I need a favor. Now, don't get upset, but I need you to go check on your dad. He called me because he has had a seizure."

My father had been an epileptic since his early adolescence. He had seizures frequently, and over the years we became accustomed to his episodes. His seizures were mostly mild, but he would have severe ones on occasion. I knew a lot about epilepsy. I knew that if he were really having seizures, he probably wouldn't have the wits about him to pick up the phone and call anyone. Besides, my Aunt Mindy lived 150 miles away.

I walked into the hallway and signaled for Daniel to mute the television. He looked at me with a confused expression, the look you give when you want to know who someone is talking to or what their conversation entails. I looked back at him like a deer in headlights.

Aunt Mindy continued, "I need you to go and check on him. Your mom is out of town, and he's alone. He told me not to call you, but I think he just didn't want to worry you."

What? What did you just say? Is this conversation real? Am I dreaming?

"Uh, I … I can't. I'm sorry, but I can't go over there. I know you don't understand, but you just have to believe me. I have my reasons. I just can't go."

Daniel was increasingly concerned. "Who is it?" he whispered.

I hushed him with a wave of my hand. I couldn't concentrate, and my mind was racing in panic.

Oh my God. What do I do? I can't go, I just can't. What are these people trying to do to me? I can't go. No … I won't go. I won't.

"Oh, well, okay. I mean, I know it's hard for you to see him that way, but someone needs to check on him."

"I know. But I just can't. Can you call Bobby or something?"

Please just shut up and call Bobby. Can't you understand I can't go over there? I won't go.

I was trembling with fear, on the verge of a panic attack. I was unprepared. I didn't know what to say. I felt that intense fight-or-flight urge again. I felt danger. I knew that I couldn't go.

Bobby had been my dad's best friend for thirty-five years. He lived five minutes away. My father could have called him, but he chose to call my Aunt Mindy and then told her *not* to call me.

"Okay, sure. I'll call Bobby."

I could hear the disappointment in Aunt Mindy's voice. Mindy is the sweetest person I've ever met in my life. The fact that I had upset her was breaking my heart. I knew that she had absolutely no idea what I was talking about.

I couldn't help but think about how awkward our conversation had been and how many questions might arise as a result. I immediately began crying as I hung up the phone. Daniel was right there to comfort me. He led me to the sofa, muted the television, and held me in his arms as I wept.

§

I went to work the next day still thinking about the night before. I couldn't get the events of the evening out of my mind and I was really upset that Aunt Mindy had seemed angry with me. I felt the need to ease her confusion, so I sent her an e-mail. I told her that I knew she didn't understand my response to her on the phone, but that I had my reasons, and I hoped that she would try to understand and respect my wishes.

She wasn't mad at me. She just thought that I didn't want to go because see him while he was having seizures was too difficult for me to watch. We exchanged several e-mails that day because she had become increasingly concerned. She just knew that something wasn't right, so she called me on my cell phone.

"Mandy, honey, what's wrong?" she asked. "What's goin' on?"

"Aunt Mindy, you don't want to know."

"Mandy, tell me what's wrong."

"I'm telling you, Aunt Mindy, you don't want to know. Please, just understand that I love you. I really don't think you want to know." I wanted so badly to protect her. But my aunt Mindy was braver than I had ever thought of giving her credit for. She vigorously pursued her instincts and questioned me without ceasing. She was determined to get to the truth.

"Honey, I need to know. Did something happen? Did he do something to you?"

"Yeah, he did."

"What did he do?"

"Trust me ... you don't want to know, Aunt Mindy."

"I have to know. Mandy, I love you. Tell me what he did?"

"Aunt Mindy, he…well…he…he abused me."

I heard a gasp of pure horror on the other end of the phone. "Did he touch you?" she asked.

"Yeah."

We were both crying. But in that moment, she did for me what my mother never could do. She loved me through the entire conversation.

"You did the right thing by telling me. You did. I'm here for you, and I love you so much. Do you hear me?"

"Yeah," I mumbled through my sniffling.

"Are you okay?"

"No. I'm not. I'm really, really not okay." I thought I was going to have a nervous breakdown right there in the break room of our office.

"Oh, honey. I am so, so sorry. Where are you?"

"I'm at work right now. I can't think. I really need to talk to you about this, but I just can't right now. I really just want to go home."

"Honey, you need to go home. Can you drive?"

"Yeah, I think so. I just need some time to calm down."

They cancelled my patients for the rest of the afternoon, and I went home.

Aunt Mindy would later share with me that she fell apart after she hung up the phone. These revelations had shattered her entire world. Everything she had thought to be real and normal was suddenly changing. She got in her car, drove to her church less than a mile away, and began walking toward the front door. She collapsed in the parking lot, wrecked with despair, and minutes later was picked up off the ground by her pastor.

He carried her inside as she continued to weep, and slowly calmed her enough to find the source of her pain. He knew exactly what to do because, unfortunately, this was a story he had heard more than a few times before. He gave her the phone number of Melinda Daniels, a fellow church member who was well versed in counseling this type of abuse. She led a group at their church for adult survivors.

Aunt Mindy drove home, and within ten minutes, Melinda was at her doorstep. Melinda immediately began to put into perspective exactly what was happening and supported Aunt Mindy in making herself strong enough to be there for me. She helped my aunt Mindy understand what a significant step I had taken in divulging my abuse to her, and what an incredible responsibility she then had to take on such a secret.

Aunt Mindy never looked back. She never once questioned her own abilities or what she should or shouldn't do. She saturated herself with knowledge and immediately took on the challenging task of advocating for me. She became my hero.

Within two hours, Aunt Mindy and Melinda Daniels called me. In that moment, I felt like this was my last hope. I felt a lot of hesitation in trusting my secrets to Aunt Mindy because of all the rejection I had already experienced with my mother. But she continually reassured me, reminding me that she wasn't going anywhere and that I could trust her. She promised me that she would not turn her back on me, and she meant every word.

I slowly began divulging the horrible secrets that I had kept for many years. She cried for me, hurt for me, felt anger for me, but most important, she loved me unconditionally. I knew that eventually my past would likely be revealed, but the explosive nature of my revelations took me by surprise. I was still very much in the bubble, but I was beginning to see that all the things I had learned to minimize were horrific to other people. The bubble was quickly deteriorating around me.

All of the mental fatigue made the day exhausting, and one that I will never forget. I knew that things were about to become acute. My confessions made me feel like someone had started a fire. Like someone had flicked a cigarette out of the window of their car and the grass caught on fire. Except this was a windy day, and the fire would spread fast, out of control. There was no way to know how long the fire would burn or how far the devastation would spread. All I could do was sit and watch the fire burn, and I had no water to put the flames out. I was helpless.

Chapter 10

The Fire Spreads

ϒ

I decided I needed to be with my Aunt Mindy. I really just wanted to skip town. I didn't want anyone coming to my house or try to pull information out of me. Daniel and I decided that the best thing for me to do would be to get away for a few days, so I could be far away when people found out. He tried his best to comfort me, but the intensity of my situation with Aunt Mindy left me feeling desperate for her physical touch and personal attention, so I left that next day and drove three hours to be with her.

I immediately felt comforted when I saw her sweet smile. She stood on the sidewalk waiting for me, and I jumped out of my car and wrapped my arms around her. I hadn't seen her in a couple of years, but she hadn't changed a bit. She had always been small boned, and her bob-cut hair was the same style she had the last time I saw her. She was over forty years old but still didn't show any gray. I could feel her love just by looking in her big chestnut eyes and seeing the excitement in her face as I arrived.

She wanted to hold me, to physically be able to comfort me. She continued to give me everything my mother could never give me and what only a woman's touch could provide.

When I arrived at her house, she had Melinda Daniels there to help guide us through the purging phase. She had already spent time counseling Mindy before I arrived, teaching her about child abuse and helping her understand how to handle everything the right way. She guided Aunt Mindy through the process of realizing her world was not as safe as it seemed and taught her how to grieve for her loss as well.

Melinda knew exactly how I was feeling and was able to help me in ways nobody else had ever done. She validated my feelings and helped me understand all these emotions and where they were coming from.

Aunt Mindy felt the need to confront my parents, but only did so with my permission. She was cautious of every single step and how her actions might affect me. She decided to call my father. She needed to hear him answer for himself, and she was determined not to just sit back and make me handle this situation on my own.

"Hey, sis," he answered.

"I *know*." She didn't want to chitchat. She wanted answers. "I know what you did."

That was all she had to say. My father sat silent on the other end.

"How could you do this to your precious little girl?"

No response.

"Answer me. Talk to me. What were you thinking?"

There was still no answer.

"Answer me."

Click.

He hung up on her, unable to answer for himself, and leaving her with the feeling of complete betrayal. They haven't spoken since that day.

Aunt Mindy had always been very close to my father, and she had to grieve for him as though he had died, much the same way I did. She never made me feel as though I was burdening her, and still, to this day, she listens and encourages me. She was met with a moral crisis, and she took the hard road.

Taking the easy road was what my mother did—ignoring, blaming, and minimizing the situation so that she didn't have to deal with the facts. But Aunt Mindy chose the hard road, the road of acceptance. She never once questioned the validity of what I was telling her. She loved me through every detail, every painstaking detail. Aunt Mindy, with Melinda's help, sat and listened to me purge the details, and not the way I'm purging now, in writing. There was something inside me that just couldn't stop.

Daniel supported me in every way I would allow, but the nature of our relationship left me hesitant to divulge any specific details of my abuse. He was, and still is, my rock. He is a man who is caring and sensitive, supportive and compassionate. He is everything opposite of my father. I didn't want any details of my abuse to interfere with the comfortable intimacy I had learned to share with him.

I needed to talk to Aunt Mindy about my childhood, because I needed someone else to know all my secrets. I couldn't live with them alone, and every detail I told her was now a detail that I shared. Sharing my secrets with Aunt Mindy was different than telling my therapist, Diana, because Diana helped me in a different way. Diana was my intellectual compass. Aunt Mindy and Melinda became my emotional compass. I needed them all.

§

Mindy's next phone call was to my mother and only a couple of hours after calling my father. My mother was still away on business and unaware that anyone had found out. I sat silent and shaking, nervously awaiting my mother's response.

"This is Mindy. How could you do what you did to your children and not believe Amanda when she tried to tell you?" She wasted no time. "How could you do that to your own children?"

"Now, Mindy, you don't understand."

"*No*! I do understand. My brother molested my niece, and you knew about it and did nothing." She was feisty in that moment, like a lioness defending her young. She never had any children of her own, but had no problems with parental instinct. She defended me.

"Mindy, this is the first I'm hearing of any of this."

"No it isn't. I know better. I know she told you, and I know you ignored it. I know everything."

"Mindy, you don't understand."

"There isn't anything you can tell me to make me not believe."

Click.

My mother hung up on her too. Aunt Mindy was finally beginning to get a true sense of my mother's and father's demeanor.

My mother immediately started damage control. She started calling people in her circle, acting as though she was in shock, like she had never heard this before. I think she wanted to be the first to tell her friends, so she could corral them with her perspective. But she was digging her own grave.

Several of her friends called me, trying their best to convince me that my mother was a victim too. On the one hand, I knew that they were only trying to help, but my mother had many people convinced that she had never heard about this before. Her friends seemed to view her as a devastated wife and mother, but I saw her as a contributor, if not an equal contributor to my abuse.

§

My second day at Aunt Mindy's house was spent much like the first. We had many moments of anger and lots of grief and comforted ourselves with big bowls of ice cream and Lifetime chick flicks.

There was one more phone call to be made before I went home the next day. Bobby and Glenda had been friends of our family and known my parents since before my brother and I were born. I grew up with their two girls and spent a lot of time with them throughout the years. Bobby had been best friends with my father for thirty-five years. I couldn't help but wonder if I had been my father's only victim.

I sat on Aunt Mindy's bed, just trembling as she dialed the numbers, and initially, the phone call did not go well.

"Bobby, this is Mindy."

"Mindy?" he asked.

"Mindy Slade."

"Oh, yeah, how are you?"

"Bobby, there is something I need to tell you. Are you sitting down? You might want to get Glenda on the phone."

"Is everything okay?"

"No. I need you to get Glenda on the phone and sit down."

"Okay. Just a minute."

He later told me that he really didn't know what to think when Aunt Mindy called. He wasn't sure if someone was hurt or dead, but nothing could prepare him for what she had to say.

"Bobby, I need you to listen to me. I know this is going to be hard to hear, but I need you just to listen to me."

"What is it?"

"Bobby, it's about Mandy and David. They were abused. Their dad abused them both, and he molested Mandy."

"What?"

"I know it's hard to hear, but he molested Mandy, and her mother knows and didn't do anything about it."

"Melinda, I can't believe that."

"I know it's hard to believe, but just think about it. It happened, and it's real, and we need to be here for these kids."

Glenda interjected, "He didn't do that. He wouldn't do that."

"Melinda, where did you hear this from?" Bobby asked.

"I know it's hard to hear, but I know that it happened. Mandy is here, and I've talked to her, and I know that it happened."

"Well, I just can't believe that. He just couldn't have done that," Bobby said.

Aunt Mindy ended the conversation with a request for them to think about the past and entertain the possibility that this had actually happened so that they could, in turn, talk to their girls and make sure they hadn't also been victimized.

I felt completely disheartened. I hated the fact that they didn't believe me, but I tried really hard not to let the rejection get me down. I left Aunt Mindy's house the next day and returned home. My visit with her was incredibly therapeutic, but I was still bothered by the fact that Bobby and Glenda didn't believe me. It didn't take long for that to change.

Shortly after I returned home that day, I received a call.

"Mandy, this is Glenda."

"Hi." The sound of her voice made me very nervous.

"Can you come over to our house? We want to talk to you and David."

"Why?" I felt panicked again.

"Bobby and I want to talk to you and David about what your Aunt Mindy discussed with us last night."

"I don't know. I mean, what do you want to discuss?"

"We've been thinking about this all day, and we just really need to hear this from the two of you."

"Is David there?" I asked.

"He's on his way right now."

"Okay. Then I'll come."

"It'll be okay. I promise," she assured me.

"Okay."

I cried all the way to their house. I was so nervous, and I really didn't think I was equipped to handle any doubtful questioning. I walked in the door, and Glenda was already crying. She tried to make me feel more comfortable by meeting me with a hug, but she was so short that I could see the top of her gray-blond hair, and the difference in height made me feel more like I was comforting her.

My brother and I sat on the couch, slumped like little children again. I felt like I was somehow in trouble. Like I was the child again getting scolded by two adults.

"There are some allegations of abuse of you two by your father. We want to hear from you that it happened," Glenda said.

"It happened," I mumbled.

"Mindy says that you were both physically abused and that you were sexually abused, Amanda. Is that true?" Bobby asked.

"It's true," I said. Tears were rolling down my cheeks, and my head was hung in shame.

Bobby is such a big guy, even bigger than my father, and I had not yet learned how to interact well with middle-aged men. I assumed that all men my father's age were a lot like my father. Plus, Bobby wore a mustache much like my father's, and I interpreted his deep voice as more authoritative than he intended.

"David, is this true? Did you know he had molested her?" Bobby asked again.

"Yes, it's true. It happened. It all happened." David hung his head to hide the tears that were welling up in his eyes.

"How do you know? I mean, are you sure?" Bobby asked.

His questions angered me "Sure? Of course I'm sure. What's that supposed to mean?" *Like I don't know for sure what happened to me. What a dumb question.*

Glenda quickly interjected to make us less uncomfortable. "He doesn't mean that. He's just in shock. He doesn't know what to say. When Melinda called us, we thought she was crazy. But as the day went on, we both kept thinking about it. I asked Bobby, 'What if it's true? What if this really did happen?' We couldn't just ignore it. We both felt like we needed to hear it from the two of you. We want both of you to know that we love you very much, and we're here for you. It's just going to take a little time to sink in."

We just sat there. Neither of us knew what to say. I couldn't stop the anxiety that was causing me to shake. I wanted to vomit from the stress. But secretly I was happy to have my brother sitting beside me. He didn't run from the truth. He stood up for me and told them, and I didn't feel alone.

I don't remember how long we were there that night, but we tried as best we could to answer their questions. Bobby and Glenda had already discussed the situation with their grown daughters and were able to rule them out as possible victims.

I called Diana on her cell phone as soon as I left. I was overwhelmed. I advised her of everything that was going on, and she made room for me in her schedule for the next day, but only after calming my anxiety. I couldn't help but think of how difficult things were going to become. Everyone was suddenly feeling the need to call and talk to me about the information they were receiving.

Daniel and Diana both continued to urge me not to answer the phone, but I ignored those requests. In my mind, every phone call gave me another chance to find some sort of clarity or understanding that I had been hoping to find.

§

Bobby wanted to hear my father answer for his own behavior. They had known each other for almost four decades, and Bobby was struggling with himself over not having seen the signs of abuse. I remember him repeatedly apologizing, desperate to take back the time and see something new that he hadn't been able to pick up on before. He wanted to save me and David, but that opportunity had long passed.

According to Bobby, he drove to my father's house while my mother was at work. When he arrived, my father came out the front door smiling, as if nothing was happening. Surely my father knew what Bobby was there for, but he still managed to pretend as though nothing was bothering him.

Bobby stepped out of his truck and approached the house, immediately announcing the purpose for his visit.

"We need to talk, and I think you know what it's about," he said.

"Come on inside," my father told him.

They went inside and sat down. My father was sitting in a chair directly facing the television, and Bobby sat to his right. Bobby said my father wouldn't make eye contact.

"Do you have any idea what you've done here?" Bobby asked him.

"I'm not going to talk about it," my father rebutted. He had no emotion, just a blank stare straight ahead, with his eyes glued to the television screen.

"Are you aware of what David and Amanda are saying you did? How could you have done this?"

"I said I'm not going to talk about it."

"I think we should talk about this. Don't you have anything to say for yourself?"

"I won't confirm it, but I won't deny it either. We're either not going to talk about it, or we're not going to talk."

"If that's the way it's going to be, then I'd better go."

Bobby was crushed. He began to get a sense of the difficulty I was having in my recovery. He felt hurt and betrayed by my father, and they haven't spoken since. Thirty-five years of friendship, and my father couldn't even answer him. Bobby and Glenda would both be nothing but strong advocates for us from that day forward.

§

I spent a lot of time with my husband at my in-laws' house during those days, just trying to be around people who supported and loved me. But one day I left and went home to be by myself. I left against their wishes and decided just to go home and lie down.

I was sitting alone in the floor of our guest bedroom. The floor was empty except for the spare dresser that fills the corner facing the doorway. There is a large double-paned window that faces the road and a sky view window above that one. My husband was still at his parents' house, and I had been home alone for thirty minutes.

The phone calls had become overwhelming and the intensity of the moment had allowed the devil to take hold of my thoughts.

I was clenching a full bottle of sleeping pills, with tears streaming down my face and feelings of hopelessness in my heart.

I can't do this anymore. I just can't.

I was crying and feeling sorry for myself, debating my options, and wondering if there was a soul in the world who *truly* loved me. At the time, I didn't know how to recognize or receive that type of deep affection. I had longed to know the feeling of unconditional love, and I was still too angry at God to allow him to fill that void in me.

The phone had been ringing nonstop with friends, family, and even acquaintances wanting to know how this could be possible.

"You don't need to be talking to these people," Daniel would say. "They don't have a clue. They're just gonna make you more upset."

I knew he was right, but curiosity kept getting the best of me. I wanted to hear what they had to say, and more important, I wanted to hear what my mother was saying to them.

I wasn't prepared for the multitude of questions, but I felt the need to defend my position. The acute stress of my revelations had become too much.

I can't do this anymore. God, please help me, I just can't do this anymore. I just don't understand this. Why, God? Why?

Even now, admitting how truly close I came to ingesting the bottle of sleeping pills is difficult. I thought about my husband coming home and finding me lying there. I thought about how the discovery would change him forever, and I couldn't do that to him. I realized the unhealthiness in my thoughts and knew that somewhere, somehow, there had to be a purpose to the suffering I was enduring.

The phone rang again, and this time it was my husband. "Honey, I really don't want you to be there alone," he said. "I'm worried about you." He said it with such compassion. I could hear the worry in his voice.

"I know. You're right. I need you here with me. I can't be alone right now. Please come home."

"I'm on my way. I love you."

"Love you too."

He turned the phone off when he arrived home and forbade me to answer any more calls. He was desperate to protect me as best he could, dancing a fine line between letting me take my own journey and keeping me from self-destruction. Daniel showed more patience than any man would be expected to have and never once made me feel like I was doing the wrong thing.

I lay down that night and thought about all the things in my life that I still wanted to achieve and how thankful I was that I hadn't taken those pills. I desperately wanted to be a mommy myself. I wanted to be able to give my children the childhood for which I had longed—to watch them grow and learn and play, knowing they were loved and wanted and safe. I longed to grow old with my husband and take walks in the park holding his hand. My eyes had been swollen for days, and my head was throbbing from all the tears I had shed. I soon drifted to sleep from all the exhaustion my emotions had caused.

I never told Diana or my husband about my suicidal thoughts. Looking back, I really should have. They could have gotten me the immediate help that I really needed, but my thoughts scared me enough at the time that I never thought about suicide again.

Chapter 11

Tape Confessions

ϒ

The old blue and red trailer was still sitting behind my parents' brick home, though it was no longer habitable. The weeds had taken over the front of the trailer, and there were no traces left of the garden that my brother and I had spent so many hours tending as children. There were many old boxes that had been packed away in the trailer, some of which hadn't been touched in years.

In late July of 2005, my mother was cleaning out the trailer and trying to gather old belongings for a garage sale, and David was helping her sort through the boxes. David called me that evening, obviously nervous and upset about events from earlier in the day.

"I was at the trailer today with Momma," he said.

"Yeah. So? What's wrong?"

"Well ... we found the tape."

"What tape? You mean *the* tape?"

"Yeah."

I really didn't know what to think. I couldn't believe that the tape had survived all these years packed away in dusty boxes during the middle of the hot summer, and resurfaced at what seemed to be the most perfect timing.

"How do you know it was the tape?" I asked.

"We listened to it."

"What do you mean you listened to it? What was on it? Wait ... no ... don't tell me. I don't want to know."

I was crying partially from embarrassment, but mostly from relief. The tape was real, and my mother had listened to it. She could no longer live in such deep denial, and she now had to acknowledge that my father had sexually abused me.

"I don't understand. How did you know it was the tape?"

"I just knew as soon as I saw it, and I gave it to Momma. She wanted to listen to it, so we got a tape player out and listened."

"Are you okay? I mean ... I know it had to be hard to hear."

"Yeah. I'm okay. I don't really want to talk about it, but I'm okay."

"Well I don't want to know what was on it anyway. I just don't think I can handle that."

"You don't need to know. It won't change anything. All you need to know is that she heard it. She knows that he did it."

I still do not know what was on that tape, and I am thankful that I never came across the tape myself. But after my mother heard the tape, she decided to destroy the contents and throw the tape in the garbage. She told me that she destroyed the tape to protect me, and that there wasn't anything audible on the tape anyway. I knew better. She destroyed that tape to protect my father.

I was furious that she had destroyed the tape, and even more furious that I had to learn about the discovery of the tape from my brother. I didn't understand how she could still be cold and disconnected even with all the evidence she had seen and heard.

She e-mailed me soon after my brother called to tell me about the tape, defending herself, and justifying her behavior. I still cry when I read her words today.

§

The things that other people are telling me … *I did not know* about. Did you *try* to tell me when you were younger? *I do not remember*!! Whether you believe me or not is your choice. There were some very stressful things going on in *my* life during that time. I am expected to be very strong. Yet I am not a strong person.

When you came to me about a year and a half ago, I do remember saying to you at that time, "I can't handle this … I am confused." You told me and your brother both that you had forgiven him, and that we were going to move forward. That was your decision, not mine. You chose that. It was after you forgave your dad that I asked you not to bring it up again. I understand that you still have flashbacks of things that happened. I wish that I could take those away from you so you wouldn't hurt anymore. I understand that you tried to go on with our family life and you just cannot handle it. I am not mad at you for any of that. I come from a family that just puts things behind them and moves on. I never realized that there are things that are harder to put behind you and that some people just can't do that.

I don't know what kind of relationship we can have. We seem to go back and forth with our relationship, but I know that I will take whatever I can get with you. My heart holds a very special place for both my children. That will never go away. It is totally up to you as to whether we have a relationship or not.

I believe that when a person can only focus on the bad times they forget the good times and that makes life hard for them. That is what I have chosen to do in my life. Now, do I get mad sometimes at things that have happened to me? Yes. Then I have to stop and remind myself that I need to focus on the positives in my life. I am only telling you how I feel about me. How I deal with things.

What makes you think I am pretending to care??? Because I didn't let you know about the tape. You know you weren't there when I heard the tape. You don't know what my reaction was. You are assuming because I did not tell you about the tape, or get hysterical like some people have that I don't care about you. You are so wrong in that assumption. Yes, this is very hard for me to comprehend that this happened to you. Yes, I do know something happened to you. I am sorry I didn't tell you sooner. I did not want to interfere with your therapy. The decision was made to wait on *your* next move. Well, you made that move when you made the decision to tell everyone. Am I pissed that this has been done to you? *Yes*, I am. Is me getting mad at the world, hysterical, going to help the situation? *No*, I don't feel like it will. I have learned over the years that getting hysterical at things only creates bigger problems. You are mad at me because I did not react like you felt I should have, I am sorry that I didn't give you the reaction that you needed me to. Did things change for me after I heard the tape, *oh*, yes they did. You don't know. You were not here.

I have asked many people about what the Bible says about molesting and abusing your children and leaving your spouse. I have not found anyone yet that can tell me where it talked about that. I would like some scriptures on that.

I am sorry that I failed you as a mother. I understand that you do not feel that you can come to me about things. I will learn to deal with that. I never realized what was going on with you. I am truly sorry. *No* I did not only care about image and how things looked.

I am very annoyed that you are assuming how I feel. You don't know how I feel; you don't know how confused I am that all this took place. Do you want me to just stop communicating with you? Do you want me to be completely out of your life? I do not want you to be out of my life. I realize there will be boundaries. I realize that I may do or say something to annoy you. Well you know what? That's life. Just as people do or say stuff to annoy me.

Love, Mom

I was angry and hurt when I read her letter. I felt like she was still trying to brainwash me. I needed her to validate my pain, but she couldn't. She was too busy trying to be right to accept the true gravity of what all had occurred. My response came just a few hours later.

I do want you to know that I do love you very much. But you seem to be very cold and distant. I want you to know that I am very angry with you because I not only tried to tell you one time, but five times that you did not acknowledge. I remember each time specifically; it just doesn't seem possible that you just all of the sudden don't remember. You have *never* tried to help me … ever. You are my mother and you have turned your back on me time and time again. None of this is new to you. This is what you have known for a very long time. If you don't remember, then you truly do need help. You absolutely turned your back on me numerous times. If my own mother doesn't believe me, who else will?

It is truly a miracle that I have turned out as functional as I have because the things I endured are too much for most people to comprehend. I feel like I am fourteen again, coming to you for help, and you are stabbing me in the back all over again. It hurts. More than you could ever imagine.

Your letter to me was all about *your* pain and *your* suffering and how stressful life has been for *you*. You just flat don't get it. You were the adult, and I was the child. It doesn't matter what very stressful things you thought you were experiencing. I can promise you my life was absolutely in turmoil, and I was the *child*, dealing with a *child* mind, and absolutely no one to turn to. If you truly do not remember the many times I tried to tell you, then you definitely need to seek help.

Whether you remember or not, this *is* what happened. Let me explain something to you. There was more than just sexual abuse here. There was mental, emotional, physical, and spiritual abuse as well. He had complete control over my mind and my will. As far as the tape, if you were so concerned when you heard the tape, why did you destroy it? It sure makes you look like you were destroying evidence. What does that say about your judgment?

You *never* asked me what happened or offered me help. You acted like I should shrug this off and move on. How can you be so *cold*? When did you ever put your arms around me and tell me how sorry you were for what happened to me? When did you ever try to help me? Why is it that everyone else can do that for me except my own mother? You can't fix this. You can't change my mind. I know what happened. You need to get help for yourself. You can't help me. You only hurt me more. I am not closing the door on you. You are the one pushing me further and further away by not even admitting what actually happened. You act so innocent in this whole deal. You are in complete denial. That tape was not yours to destroy. You should have at least held on to it.

You need to learn about the mind of a child molester. You need to learn about the statistics. Will you *ever* get it? I truly don't know. I hope so. I really hope so.

Amanda

My mother and I were unable to agree on anything. We continued to argue back and forth, each defending our position, and we got nowhere. The more we discussed the past, the further apart we seemed. I wanted her to admit what she had done and how damaging her denial had been for me, but she was determined to defend herself. Every interaction with her had become toxic. I started to think that she might never be able to give me what I needed from her.

Chapter 12

Gift of Life

ℵ

I first realized I had missed my period in the beginning of August of 2005. The stresses that I had been under made me ignore any instinct to believe I could be pregnant. I was not mentally prepared for pregnancy, but the thought did bring a touch of excitement. I decided not to tell anyone until I could take a home pregnancy test.

I bought a couple of cheap tests, the kind that have two lines if you're pregnant, one if you're not. But I also bought a digital test because it was much more dependable, with no room for misinterpretation. The window of the test would either say "pregnant" or "not pregnant" after only a minute of waiting.

I came home and rushed to the bathroom. I took all three tests, but focused in on the digital one since the results would come much faster than the line tests. That minute was the longest minute of my life. I was sitting on the edge of the bathtub with my head down between my legs counting in my head from one to sixty. Then I eased my eyes to the counter and read the results.

"Pregnant."

Daniel and I had been wanting a child, so I knew that this pregnancy was going to bring much joy to our lives, but the timing didn't exactly seem perfect. Regardless of the timing, I knew that I needed this child, and God knew I needed her too. I couldn't wait to tell Daniel.

He had built up enough seniority at the police department to move to midnight shift, an improvement on the evening shift that had kept us apart for much of the week. But his new shift made him sleep during the day, so several hours passed before he woke up to hear the news.

I heard the television turn on in the bedroom, and I knew he was trying to wake up. I walked into the room and instantly announced,

"Babe, I have something to tell you."

He muted the television and sat up. "What is it honey?"

"Well ..." I was grinning from ear to ear, unable to find the appropriate words to tell him.

"What's goin' on?"

I pulled the pregnancy test from behind my back, and his face lit up.

"Are you pregnant?" he asked.

I just nodded yes.

"I knew you were pregnant. I just knew it."

"How did you know?"

"I just sensed it, I guess. You've been acting so different. I can't even explain it really, other than I just knew."

We sat and hugged each other, fantasizing over baby names and making fun of each other's suggestions. We went to his parents' house and told them we were expecting, and the news just continued to spread from there.

I was overwhelmed with excitement and contentment. I called Diana and shared the news with her. I knew she probably didn't think this pregnancy had come at the best of times either, but of course she expressed her happiness for me. A few days passed, and I met with her for another session.

"Well, how are you feeling?" She was smiling as she asked me.

"I'm good. I feel a little bit queasy sometimes, but, you know, it's to be expected. I have decided to stop taking my medicine. I don't want to be on any medications while I am pregnant."

"I understand that. Just be sure to tell your doctor that you stopped taking them."

"I already told the nurse."

"Good."

"She said it was fine if that's what I wanted, but that there were meds they could give me while I was pregnant if I needed them.

"Perfect.

"I really think I can handle this. I do. If it becomes overwhelming, I will take something. I promise."

"That's totally your decision. It's your body, and only you can say how you're feeling."

The truth was that I had never felt better. I had so much hope and so much to live for that I felt an obligation to try harder. This was just what I had needed.

"Well, do you know how far along you are?"

"No, but I go to the doctor next week to find out. I think I am probably about six or seven weeks along. I am worried, though, you know, about how this will affect the progress I have made."

At this point in my therapy, I no longer felt the need to say one thing while thinking another. I had learned to accept "the abused" as a part of myself, and I felt no need to keep that part of me separate. I was comfortable enough with Diana that I could say literally anything to her and still feel safe.

She didn't judge me or tell me my feelings weren't adequate or appropriate. She genuinely wanted to help me make a better life for myself.

"How do you think it will affect your progress?" she asked.

"I'm not sure. It just worries me that people will think, 'Oh now she's pregnant,' and somehow that's supposed to be some kind of magical cure."

"I would think it might actually help you make *more* progress." She always had a way of turning things into something positive.

"I definitely feel a lot of impending pressure. It feels like somehow I have to figure this whole thing out in the next nine months."

"What goals do you have that you feel pressured to meet?"

My mother would often flip-flop, acknowledging my abuse one minute, and the next saying she didn't know what to believe. Her reaction was completely unpredictable, and her ability to sympathize seemed nonexistent. I didn't feel comfortable trusting her with my emotions.

"Well, I feel like my relationship with my mother has to be somehow fixed before the baby comes, and I don't think that's possible. I mean, it's been in the ditch for so long, and if she can't believe me, then how do I move forward? I know she has her own counselor, but she's only doing it because it makes her look better to other people. She has never tried to get counseling before. It makes me so mad. She plays this little game where she only cares about what looks good to other people. She's trying to tell people that she never knew about all this, and it's the first time she's ever really heard what happened. It pisses me off. What about me? When has she ever cared about me?" My voice started to crack talking about my mother.

"Would you be open to having a joint therapy session with her?"

"Maybe. I don't know. I guess I haven't really thought about it. I'm not really sure what I want to do."

"What would be your best-case scenario?"

"Probably, I would love to think that my mother would actually get it. That she would come to the point where she could accept what has happened to me, no matter what she chooses with her marriage. I need for her to validate my feelings. I need for her to have sympathy for me and to understand what all I have been through."

"So, that would be best-case scenario. What would be your worst-case scenario?"

"I think my worse case would be if I try and try, and she never really gets it. It would crush me. I really need that from her. It's like a hundred people could validate my feelings, but I still need my mother to get it. That doesn't change."

"How do you see yourself trying to achieve that?"

"Well, I know that I want to be able to walk away from this whole thing, knowing that I have done everything that I possibly can to help her. I don't want to walk away wondering if I could have done more. I love my mom, and I need her, but I can't have a relationship with her if she can't talk and accept this. It is so much a part of who I am and who I have become, and we can't have a relationship that pretends that it never happened. That is exactly what I am trying to get away from. I just can't live like that anymore."

"I know her therapist, and he is going to be very objective about the situation. Is that something you want to consider?"

"I don't know. That really scares me, because I don't know him. I don't know if I can handle sitting there, having her accuse me of being a liar, and having her therapist back her up. I just don't know if I can put myself through that."

"I really don't think it would be that way at all. He's not going to form that kind of an opinion or do anything to hurt your progress. We don't have to participate in joint therapy with her, but I think you should at least think about it and keep that option open. Whatever you feel comfortable with. This is totally up to you."

"I'll think about it, but I'm just not ready to do that yet. I don't really know how to reach her yet. It all just feels like such an acute situation, and I need time to sort out my thoughts."

"That's perfectly okay. I definitely think that you shouldn't feel rushed to do anything. You've made an amazing amount of progress in a very short time. You've done in half a year what would take most people two years or more. I think you're doing a fantastic job."

"I want to be able to enjoy my pregnancy, and I don't want to be so stressed out that it affects my baby."

"We certainly need to take that into consideration. I think you're going to be okay. I wouldn't say that if I didn't mean it."

"I hope so. Sometimes I think, 'I can do this, and I'll be fine. No matter what, I'll be okay,' and other times I'm not so sure. I feel so lucky to have wonderful support from others, but they can't fix it for me. It is something I have to figure out for myself, and sometimes they don't understand that. They are so caught up in trying to fix it."

"Wouldn't you say that most people in your life are there to support you rather than trying to fix it? I mean, there may be one or two who want to try and fix this situation, but mostly people are very supportive of you, right?"

"Well, yeah, I guess so. You're right. It just irritates me, but you're right. Most everyone is letting me work this out for myself and just supporting me through it."

"It's important that you keep a good perspective about things like that so that you keep things realistic. Try not to overreact about the things that are bothering you, and focus on the things that are going well. That way, you won't be overwhelmed when those people do try to contact you and want to fix it. You can just tell them straightforward, but nicely, 'You know, I know that you want to try and fix this situation, but you can't. You can love me through it and support me, but it is something that I have to figure out for myself.'"

"I really didn't think of it like that, but I can do that. I can stand up for myself. I don't want to make anyone mad, but I have to think about what is going to be in my best interest."

"Exactly. You're doing well. And I am so happy for your pregnancy. I know that you are going to be an excellent mom. It may make you realize even further what all you have been through, but you will be such a good mother because of everything you are doing for yourself."

"Thank you. I sure hope so."

I now had another life inside of me. I was responsible for another human being, and that responsibility gave me the strength that I needed to take good care of myself mentally and physically. (Diana recently revealed to me that she was glad I got pregnant when I did. She knew that the pregnancy would be good for me, and she felt that the timing *was* perfect.)

She began to schedule another appointment for me, but she wanted to see me after a few days this time, instead of a week. I was thankful. I really needed to talk to her, and one week seemed far away. She knew exactly what I needed.

I continued to see her twice a week for several months.

Chapter 13

Work in Progress

ϒ

I spent a lot of time thinking about how I was going to handle my mother. She still had a lot of psychological control over me, and even as an adult, I found myself feeling like a child around her. She would forever be my superior, and despite the poor decisions she made regarding my brother and me, I still felt the need to be respectful. I didn't want to hurt her, and I truly hoped to help her understand what her husband had done to me. But I didn't know how to reach her.

Finally, I agreed to have joint counseling with her, deciding that would be the safest way to emotionally approach my issues with her. I knew that I would have people there to mediate my interaction with her, and she wouldn't be able to control me as much while in the company of others.

We met together, mostly in the evenings, in a small town about thirty minutes away. Her therapist shared office space with a local lawyer, and we met in the conference room for our sessions. The room was small, with a glass table set up for four people and a few extra chairs that lined the walls. The smell of cleaning solution and air freshener was always potent, as if housekeeping had just finished working in there, and sometimes peppermints were in a small bowl on the table.

Diana and I usually arrived first and sat together waiting for my mother. We would sometimes speak of our plans last minute, and she would always calm me before our session started.

"Remember," she'd remind me every time, "if it gets too much to handle, just say you need a break, and we'll stop."

I tried really hard to make my mother feel comfortable at our first meeting. I brought my ultrasound pictures and hugged her as she arrived. I was nervous. I wanted her to get what *she* had done to me. I needed her to understand that *she* had played an active role in my abuse by neglecting to act on my behalf. But our first session was a bitter disappointment.

My mother did not budge from her position. I spoke about the things my father had done to me and confronted her about her denial. She continued to say that she couldn't remember me ever telling her about the abuse, and that she still wasn't sure about exactly what happened.

I progressed in my pregnancy as our sessions continued. I started to realize that breaking free from her denial would be more difficult for her than losing me as a daughter. I was clinging to my relationship with her, forcing the niceness in our interactions in a desperate attempt to salvage what little connection I still felt toward her. Though our therapy didn't produce many positive results, we were able to set up boundaries for our relationship.

"What boundaries do you need, Amanda, in order to build a relationship with your mother?" her therapist asked.

"It's really important to me that she ..."

"Look at her and tell *her* what you need," Diana interrupted.

"I don't want you to talk about your husband. I don't want you to talk about him as though he is still my dad."

I no longer referred to him parentally, addressing him by his first name in all my conversation. Using his name in such a detached way was difficult at first. This form of separation made me feel like I was betraying him. My mind would echo his voice saying, "Honor your father and mother." Diana had to spend time reassuring me that I wasn't a bad person and that detaching myself from him would be healthy. She was right. Changing my speech was another pinhole in the complex layering of the bubble.

"You can do whatever you want with your marriage," I continued "But when you mention him to me and especially when you talk about him like he's still my dad, it just messes me up."

My mother seemed offended by my request.

"Tell her what you mean when you say 'messed up,'" her therapist said.

"It's like it triggers flashbacks and makes me really nervous because I don't know how to react."

"Tell her what those flashbacks do to you," Diana prompted.

"When you talk about him like he's still my dad, sometimes it takes me back to those moments, and it makes me feel like I am ten years old again, being abused and rejected all over again."

"Well I can't guarantee you that I won't talk about him. I mean, I'm only human," my mother remarked.

"How can you say that, knowing what all he's done to me? If you know how important this is to me, then you *can* do it."

"I'm just saying, I'll probably slip up now and then."

"But I don't understand, why would you slip up? If everyone else can be so careful and conscious of what they say, why can't you?"

"I have to walk on eggshells around you already. I just can't guarantee that I won't mess up and talk about him."

"I'm not asking you to walk on eggshells. I just don't understand why you would want to hurt me like that. If you know it hurts me when you do that, why would you?"

My mother's therapist interrupted to try, on my behalf, to explain the significance of my request. "Do you understand that every time you try to pretend like none of this happened, it devastates Amanda?"

"I guess I don't understand," my mother replied. "All I can do is try my best."

I felt like our conversation just wasn't getting through to her, but I left the office that day hopeful that she would truly try her best to maintain the boundaries. I advised her that she would only have supervised visitation of her grandchild at my house and requested that she come to the hospital only after my daughter was born. That would be our last therapy session together.

§

I delivered a precious baby girl, named Grace, at 2:05 PM on Monday, May 1, 2006. She arrived three weeks early but still managed to weigh over seven pounds. She was born with a full, thick head of dark hair that had blond highlights scattered throughout. Her lips were a perfect copy of Daniel's, and her eyes were definitely from me.

She not only changed my life—as all first babies do—she changed my perspective and my self-value. She brought me one step closer to becoming who I really was. I was a mom. I had a deep understanding of exactly what that meant for me as a person. If God could entrust me to take care of this wonderful human being, then I, too, must have worth.

Some people believed that having a baby would somehow magically heal my relationship with my mother, but they were wrong. As I adapted to motherhood, I became even more confused about our relationship because I came to understand what being a mother was all about. I certainly could not comprehend how she could be passive in her feelings toward me or my suffering. Trying to put myself in her shoes, I imagined hearing my daughter tell me, for the first time, that my husband had violated her. I couldn't understand why she didn't protect me.

Nevertheless, our relationship settled into something manageable. She would call every couple of months and come to see my daughter. She'd bring toys and clothes and enjoy her for a few hours, and we wouldn't hear from her again for several months. Every time she came over, she'd mention my father. She always had to make a point to mention what he'd been doing or how they went on vacation together.

Even when I was delivering my daughter, she tried to bring *him* to the hospital. David and Daniel prevented her from bringing him, and she still doesn't know that they told me. I let her actions at the hospital slide past me, in an effort to keep the peace. Looking back, I shouldn't have let her do that to me. I should have stood my ground from the very beginning. I couldn't believe she had the gall to try to do that to me, especially while I was in labor. But I wanted to have a relationship with her, in whatever dose I could handle, no matter how abbreviated.

I had done a lot to distance myself from the bubble, but every interaction with her was one more tug back in. I tried my best to disengage. I tried to be happy and focus on my daughter and my husband, but I knew that I had still not completely healed.

§

In January of 2007, I decided to start going back to church. I was really only going for my daughter, and I sat there week after week, expecting to be disappointed. I was not seeking God, but rather the proof of hypocrites to fulfill the views that I had already decided were factual.

Even in my early adulthood, away from church, I thought of myself as a Christian. But I was definitely cold and distant, rejecting any point of view that included vague explanations of the intense and damaging abuse that I had survived. I desperately wanted the closeness I had once felt with God, but I didn't even know where to begin to get back to that place. I often wondered if I would ever be whole again.

After six months of regular attendance, my walls began to break down. I realized that my spirit was still incomplete. I had never tried to deal with the spiritual abuse that had occurred, and I was terrified to even try. I became a Christian when I was sixteen years old, but had drifted far away. I really wanted and needed spiritual healing, but the spiritual confusion I was feeling made this aspect of healing feel very complicated.

My father used the scripture and the church to justify his behavior. Two of his favorites were:

> Children, obey your parents because you belong to the Lord, for this is the right thing to do. "Honor your father and mother." This is the first of the Ten Commandments that ends with a promise. And this is the promise: If you honor your father and mother, "you will live a long life, full of blessing." (Ephesians 6:1–3)

> If you refuse to discipline your children, it proves you don't love them: if you love your children, you will be prompt to discipline them. (Proverbs 13:24)

He interpreted these scriptures to mean that I must obey his every command, no matter what that request entailed. When he would beat us, he would always say "Spare the rod, spoil the child. I'm only doing this because I love you." Though he was clearly confused about the scripture, using his altered interpretation of the Bible was an easy way for him to justify his abuse. These are, perhaps, two of the most abused scriptures in the Bible.

He wasn't even religious until he got around other people, or until he could use religion to justify his behavior. But as a child, I'd had those misinterpretations pounded into my head so many times that I found exploring religion at all as an adult to be difficult.

My father not only failed me emotionally, physically, mentally, and sexually, but spiritually as well. God entrusted my father to raise me to his authority, and he abused that power in every aspect of his life. I thought that God had failed me. I thought that he was unjust, unloving, judgmental, impatient, unkind, and unsympathetic. I believed all of those things because those are the characteristics that my father taught me about himself. Because he portrayed himself to be such a Christian man and authorized by God, I couldn't understand how a God like that could love me, and frankly I wanted no part of a Christianity that I felt involved the hypocrisy that my father had taught me.

I became friends with our pastor's wife, Angie. She would sit and listen to my struggles and pray for me, never once judging my feelings or making me feel inadequate. She let me know I was entitled to my feelings but that God was there waiting for me, if I would open my heart to him. I wanted to believe that, but I didn't know how.

My friend Angie always had the right words to say to me. She guided me spiritually and allowed me the chance to express how I was really struggling. She still does. I didn't feel the need to tell her what I thought she wanted to hear. The ability to be candid with her was extremely important to me. I knew that God had given me her friendship and placed her in my life at the perfect time. Things wouldn't have been the same if I had met her even one year earlier.

I wanted to embrace the suffering and pain I had endured so that I could find a way to help others. I continued my spiritual journey by praying for guidance and reexploring the Bible for myself. I still don't have all the answers, but peeling back the spiritual layers was easy because I had already healed mentally and emotionally.

I began to understand the demands I was placing on God. We, as humans, want to be individuals and have our freedom and then we blame God when things don't work out the way we envision. I learned that God would have never ordained the suffering I endured but that he would love to be the source of my healing. At that point, I realized God was molding me into a different person. I began to feel like the person I always knew I should have been.

§

Even with all of the work I had done, the anxiety that was within me was irrepressible. I didn't quite understand why I was still displaying physical symptoms of PTSD even though I had made so much progress in my healing. I really wanted to be able to control the anxiety on my own, but I made an appointment with my doctor and decided to discuss my symptoms with him.

The nurse practitioner who had been such a key player in my decision to start counseling had since moved on to another city and had transferred all my records to one of the doctors in her old practice. He had a whole file on my history, including correspondence from my counselor on the progress that I had made.

I knew that I never wanted to be back in that place of depression I had been in for all those years. So I reluctantly disclosed the anxiety that I was still experiencing. I broke down in tears because I felt, in that moment, that somehow I had failed. I had failed to change the physical symptoms of my PTSD, and I needed help.

"Hey, Amanda. Tell me what's going on." He had an impeccable bedside manner. He was sympathetic and sensitive to my situation.

"I wanted to talk to you about maybe getting back on some medicine for my anxiety."

"Well, tell me some of your symptoms," he said.

"I think I'm experiencing more anxiety than depression. Sometimes I just start shaking, like right now. I try not to, but I can't stop it on my own."

"I think that depression and anxiety go hand in hand, but the symptoms you're having can easily be helped with the right medication."

"I know, but I really didn't want to have to take any medication. I wanted to be able to control this on my own."

"Amanda, you have to understand that this isn't a failure on your part."

"But will I need the medicine forever? I've done so much work to better myself, and still I need medication."

"If you do, then you do. What's happened here is not your fault. Your body is so hardwired to be anxious that it doesn't really know how not to be at this point. You've lived in such a high-anxiety environment for so long, and through the formative years. During times of stress, your brain releases certain chemicals, and you can't just shut that off. That is the way your brain was trained to function. Medication can really help with the physical symptoms of anxiety that you are experiencing."

"Okay, I'll try it. I really don't want to go backward, because I am still making progress, even today."

"How about this? I'll start you off on the lowest dose, and I'll see you back in a month to see how well it's working."

"Okay. Sounds like a plan."

Upon reflection, I did exactly what I needed to do by telling him that I was struggling. I had to humble myself to the realization that I had a chemical imbalance, and that I had not failed as a person. The medication definitely helped my anxiety. I was proud of myself. I had finally learned the boundaries of my own capabilities.

Chapter 14

Saying Good-Bye

I had been doing very well since the baby was born, and I had only seen Diana a few times in the previous year. I hadn't talked to her in probably six months when she returned an urgent message I left her in January of 2008.

"Amanda, this is Diana. I got your message. What's going on?"

I was crying uncontrollably and shaking as I spoke. "I really need to talk to you. Can I come in sometime this week?"

"Are you okay? What's going on?" She was genuinely concerned.

"I really don't want to talk about it on the phone. I'm really upset. Can I come to talk to you? It's about my mom. Please, I just need to talk to you."

"Yeah … Let me see what I have available."

"She wrote me this e-mail that I don't even understand. It's crazy. And she said something to me at Christmas, and I just really can't think right now, I'm so upset. I don't really want to talk about it on the phone."

"Can you come tomorrow morning at 10:30?"

"I'll be there."

"Will you be okay until then?"

"If I've made it this far, I can make it till tomorrow morning."

"Okay. I'll see you tomorrow."

I cried all evening and tried to understand my mother's flawed logic. I walked into Diana's office the next morning with my eyes swollen, no makeup, and my hair pulled back looking like I had just literally stepped out of bed and put my shoes on. I was clenching my purse in one hand and the folded printout of her e-mail in the other. I couldn't wait to see Diana. She had become my safe zone and such an important part of my healing. I knew that she would help me see things logically and allow me to feel the emotions I was experiencing, without judgment.

"Hey there." Her voice was always uplifting, and she always greeted me with a smile.

"Hey." I stood up and walked in, without even looking her in the face. I was already weeping.

"What happened?"

"It's my mom."

"Oh, sweetie, what happened?"

"I can't do this anymore. I can't fight with her anymore."

"Tell me what happened."

"It's so many things. I don't know where to start."

"Just tell me what you're thinking."

I couldn't talk to her. I was distraught. I cried, and I wept. I sat there thinking about all the years of hurt that had developed between my mother and me. Diana sat silently, just waiting for me to regain my composure enough to speak.

"It all started back at my daughter's birthday party."

"Okay."

"My mom came, for like thirty seconds."

"I don't understand."

"She walked in the door, set the presents down, and said she forgot something in her car. She left. She left without saying happy birthday, or good-bye. She left for no reason."

"How did you know she left?"

"My brother told me when he came. He pulled me into the garage and told me that she didn't feel comfortable, so she went home. I had put so much effort into making her feel welcome, but she just left."

"How did you feel?"

"I was devastated. I was standing in the garage crying, with everyone inside my house waiting for a birthday party. It took away all of the happiness from Grace's first birthday. I really didn't want to fight with her, so I just sent her an e-mail thanking her for the presents and inviting her to come back by, if she got the chance. We never spoke about it. It wouldn't have done any good."

"You did the right thing, it wasn't worth fighting about. It wouldn't have solved anything anyway. What happened after that?"

"After the party, every time we would talk, she'd find a way to mention him. She'd mention his name, or drop a line in her e-mails about what he was doing that day. It makes me so mad because she knows she isn't supposed to do that."

"It sounds like she is testing the boundaries."

"That's exactly how I feel. It's like I would cry when I didn't hear from her for a while, but then when I did, I would end up crying and mad too. I knew she would come over at Christmas, so I tried to put it behind me and enjoy the time I had with her. That's when she ..."

My heart was aching to the point that I moaned with pain. My mom had truly hurt me.

"Take your time, Amanda. What did she do?"

"She came over the day after Christmas to bring some toys. When she got ready to leave, she sat down in front of me on the coffee table and … I feel so stupid right now. Look at how upset I am."

"She hurt you. You have every right to be upset. Tell me what happened."

"She said, 'You know that I love you.' I said I love you too. Then she leaned into me and said, 'You know … these presents are from your dad, too.'"

"I'd like to say I'm shocked," Diana said, "but I don't think anything could shock me at this point. What did you say?"

"She kept talking, but I couldn't hear anything she was saying. Everything was just really hazy, and I couldn't believe she had just said that. I really don't remember what happened after that until she left. When she walked out the door, I just broke down crying. She was mad, I guess, because I didn't respond to what she had said. I guess she thought I'd just say, 'Oh, they're from him too. Well, okay, that makes everything just fine.' I mean, what was she thinking, saying something like that? Why would she do that to me?"

"I think what is happening here is that there has been a good amount of time that has passed, and she feels comfortable enough to test those boundaries."

"But why would she? Doesn't she know what that does to me?"

"I don't think she does. She is still in denial at the gravity of this situation, and somewhere inside of her she thinks she can still make it all go away."

"As dumb as it sounds, I even ignored that. I didn't mention it because I desperately wanted her just to drop it. I kept thinking, *If I keep ignoring her, she will stop.* But she keeps going further and further."

"Exactly. Because every time you ignore her, she thinks she can push you a little bit further."

"Then I got this e-mail from her a week ago, and it's just crazy. She started off nice, then ripped into me a little, and ended with niceness again. She seems to think she can say whatever she wants to me as long as her hurtful words are sandwiched with kindness."

I handed Diana the e-mail and put my head down between my legs, sobbing. I was crying so hard that I couldn't speak.

§

January 9, 2008

Hey there,

Just checking on y'all. Hope y'all are doing good.

Has Grace cooked anything good on her new kitchen set? I do hope she is enjoying it. It is such a neat kitchen.

You know Mandy I do have a phone, cell phone and work phone. You can call your mom sometimes. I don't know if you have even realized it or not or maybe you just don't care, but you never call me. I love you and your family so very much. And while I am on a roll here, have you ever made an attempt to take Grace to see your Memaw? I believe the last time she saw her was when she came to the hospital when Grace was born, unless my information is wrong. I really don't think it is right for her to be fussed at all the time about being in touch with you. When have you made an attempt to get in touch with her? I know that she has called you. Just think about it. It is totally up to you what you do. You can't wait around for people to get in touch with you. You have to make an effort too. I just needed to say my piece.

I do love you so very very much.

Mom

§

Several minutes passed before I could muster enough composure to talk about my feelings. That e-mail felt like the straw that broke the camel's back. I wasn't so much upset over the e-mail, rather the accumulation of events that the words in her note seemed to compound.

"I just can't do this anymore. I can't fight anymore. I am a different person, and I just literally don't have any more fight left in me. She can't just act like she's my mom when she wants to and then ignore me when I need her."

"Amanda, you have gone above and beyond what anyone would expect to try and build a relationship with her."

"But I don't even understand where this is coming from. Everything has been fine, and we've been getting along. Why would she try to cause more trouble between us? I literally don't even know what she's talking about with my grandmother. I've never even been close to her."

"Is that her mom or his?"

"It's his mom, and she lives a block away from them. I've never been close to her in my whole life. They always kept me away from her and talked bad about her, and all of the sudden *I'm* the bad person. It's just crazy. I'm not gonna go visit someone who lives a block away from the man that terrorized me for years. Why can't she get that?"

"She's not capable. At some point, you have to accept the fact that you've done everything you can."

"I know I have. But it hurts. It hurts so badly. I can't even explain to you how bad."

"Of course it does. It's your mom."

"It's like, at this point, she doesn't even realize what she is doing. She can't win, so she'll go down fighting. I just can't fight with her anymore. I can't."

"You shouldn't. Your mom is at the point now where she really just needs a miracle."

"I hate that. I really hate it. I tried so hard, and I really wanted her to get it. I wanted her to stick to the boundaries we set so we could at least talk. But she is so toxic."

"You're right. She *is* toxic. For the moment, she doesn't see any other way to be. Did you respond to her?"

"No. I can't. Right now, I just don't even want to talk to her. I can't."

"I think that is a good decision. I think that, above all, you need to focus on regaining your confidence and grieving over the situation. I think it's over. You've done everything you wanted to do to try and help, and right now you need to just grieve that."

"Daniel said that he can't stand to see me hurt anymore. He said that this is it. He doesn't want me to talk to her because she isn't capable of letting it go. I know that he is right. I've known for a long time, but it is so hard to accept."

"I think Daniel is right. He has sat back and supported you through this whole thing, and now he is saying, as your husband, enough is enough."

"I really didn't want this. Do you remember when you asked me about my best-case scenario and my worst case?"

"Yeah."

"It's like, you say those things, but you're so hopeful for the best case and you'll settle for anything in between. You don't really think it will end up being the worst case, you know?"

"I understand. But Amanda, things are going really well for you in your life right now. You have a good job and a wonderful husband and daughter, and you've been happy. You can't let this continue to bring you down."

"I know. But I just can't even talk to her. I love her so much, but I can't even talk to her. That seems so strange. She needs a true awareness of exactly what has happened and her role in this. I don't trust her. I think that she will hurt me again and again and continue to have no ownership in it."

"I think you're right. What do you plan to do for the rest of the day?"

"Well, I really need to talk to my friend Angie. She is the pastor's wife, and I've become friends with her. I talk to her about a lot of things, and she helps me spiritually and prays for me. I really need to go see her and ask her some questions."

"I think that's a good idea. I don't think it's good for you to be alone. Why don't you and Daniel spend the evening at his parents' house? It'll help keep your mind off things."

"Okay. We can do that."

"Good. So you have a plan. You call me if you need anything or if anything else happens. I want to see you again next week. Can you come in on Thursday at the same time?"

"Yeah. I'll be here."

"I mean it. You call me if you need me."

"I will."

The clock showed only one o'clock and Grace was still at her babysitter's house, so I left and went to see Angie. I sat in her living room and poured my heart out to her for several hours. I wept and I cried. She held me and hugged me and listened to every word I had to say. She prayed for me to have guidance and wisdom, and I felt comforted. I knew that I had literally no more fight left in me. My anger had melted into hurt, and my defenses were weak with pain.

I cried nonstop the entire weekend. I was grieving for the loss of a dream, the loss of our relationship, and the thought that my mother would probably never choose to step out of her denial. The reality was unbearable.

I tried to go to work on Monday morning, but I was completely grief-stricken. I felt like this was the final chapter in the life of my abused self. I had made many difficult choices to better myself, but this one I found particularly difficult. I still love my mom. I will always hold out hope for her. And I would want nothing less than for her to come to me one day, with no prompting, only guilt, and tell me with sincerity that she understands how her choices have affected my life. I will never ever stop loving her, but I cannot have a relationship with her as long as she chooses to stay sick.

My husband and I decided to send her an e-mail, from *him*, to let her know she had crossed the line one too many times. I became ill with sadness and literally unable to function. I was having a nervous breakdown. That e-mail was, by far, the most difficult letter I had ever written in my life. The grief of the entire situation, all coming together in one moment, was overwhelming. I felt like I was not only saying good-bye to my mom, but

I was also saying good-bye to everything that represented the bubble. I was saying good-bye to "the abused."

§

Because of some recent events, I feel it is time for me to step in and protect my wife and family. I've always tried to allow Amanda to handle this situation how she felt necessary. But over the last three years I've seen her repeatedly hurt, and many times on the verge of a nervous breakdown.

I've been the one who has been there to pick her up when she has horrendous nightmares, flashbacks, and overwhelming and often debilitating anxiety. I know that Amanda loves you very much as do I, but she suffers from Post Traumatic Stress Disorder and can no longer be placed in this situation.

When you and Amanda had joint therapy to try and build a relationship, there were specific boundaries you were asked not to cross. The most important boundary was that you do not bring his name up. That you don't tell her how he is doing or what he is doing or even mention his name. Clearly you are incapable of maintaining that boundary and have violated it many times.

I'm not sure if you just can't see the tremendous amount of damage that has been done to her, or if you are just in denial. The comment you made at Christmas about the toys being from him too, and the e-mail you sent last week were incredibly insensitive and hurt her once again.

I have seen Amanda go above and beyond what any rational person would be expected to do in order to maintain a relationship with you. She wanted so desperately for you to get it, to understand this trauma and the seriousness of its effects on a person's mind.

Amanda has survived the most awful thing that can happen at the hands of her own father. She survived his molestation, his physical abuse and mental torment. Not only that, but she has survived the secret. The secret that she was forced to keep for so many years. Amanda has become a thriving, independent, loving, caring mother and wife despite all the horrible things that she has endured. Out of her love for you as her mother she chose not to pursue certain legal actions.

The stress that is caused by even the utterance of his name and e-mails that are of an attacking nature are causing her to have a nervous breakdown. After seeking counsel of two independent therapists, Amanda and I have come to the conclusion that this relationship is too toxic to continue.

Love was not a factor in this decision, it was lack of cooperation. It is our hope that one day you will be able to grasp the amount of damage that has been done and what a strong and awesome person she is to have overcome it. I know that you love your daughter, but you are not able to give her what she needs to be healthy. This being said, the only way for Amanda to remain healthy is for you both to just love each other from a distance.

Daniel

Chapter 15

After Silence

ϒ

It is now September of 2008, and I feel like I am a completely different person today. I will always grieve for my child self, and I have moments when I just break down and cry. Sometimes the pain is still overwhelming, but I allow myself the permission to grieve, and then I move on and continue my life. I will never "get over" what happened to me, because that is so much a part of what made me the person I am today. I will always hold out hope for my mother, but I no longer feel responsible for saving her.

When I think of all the people who have touched my life, I am truly humbled. I still live in the same town where I grew up, and occasionally I run into people I haven't seen in years. Their queries about my family are still sometimes painful, but they help remind me of how far I've come. I am now able to respond politely by saying, "I'm not sure if you're aware of this, but I actually don't have a relationship with my parents any longer." Sometimes they will ask questions, and I answer candidly, but most of the time, just hearing about the absence of communication is enough to make the questioner back away.

In telling my story, I did experience the end of relationships with family members or friends who could not deal with the gravity of abuse that occurred. You really do find out who your true friends and family are when something terrible happens. I was certainly not the only person hurt by my father's actions. He was considered to be an upstanding citizen, a contributing member of society, and a religious family leader. He devastated an entire community.

I have gained a loving and supportive circle of people around me that has filled me with an unconditional love that I never felt before. They truly helped me make myself whole again and become the woman I was always meant to be.

Thinking about what my life would be like today, if I had not completely escaped from "the bubble," is scary. As a mother, I could never knowingly allow my daughter to be in the hands of a molester, because then I would be victimizing her. I would take this same journey again a thousand times just to save her. I can, at least, have comfort in knowing that I took the right steps to make myself a better mother and that I will never have to worry about my daughter becoming a victim of his sickness.

I now have a relationship with God that fills a void and no longer makes me feel like an orphan. I'm reminded about the story of the footprints in the sand. Thinking that God has abandoned us in our desperate times is easy, but, looking back, I see how many ways he carried me through. I think about the imagination he gave me that enabled me to escape into a different world, if only for a little while. He allowed me the protection of shutting my reality off in times of extreme trauma, and he opened doors for me that I chose to walk through time and time again.

He gave me the intelligence to do well in school so that I could have a way out. I think about people like Phillip, my youth minister, placed in my life to pray for me and guide me, even though he and many others didn't know what they were praying for.

He gave me a wonderful husband and amazing in-laws who have shown me Christ's love and helped me understand that some people are exactly as they appear to be. He led me to the door of a nurse practitioner who picked up on clues of desperation and then sent me to a counselor I could entrust with my deepest, darkest secrets. He gave me the strength to stand up for what's right and the tools to be able to do so.

He gave to me another precious life to take care of and showed me how worthy I was to enjoy her. And he led me to my church home where I met my friend Angie, who prayed for me even when I didn't want to be prayed for and guided me through the complications of the spiritual abuse to help me see the other side.

As for my brother, David, he is now a happily married, successful professional and a kind and compassionate human being. He, too, has overcome the legacy of abuse. He has always encouraged my healing and has supported every decision I've made along the way. We will always be close to each other.

As I sit here today, I am a confident, loving, sensitive, and caring person, a privileged mother, and a gracious wife. God created me to be this way from birth, but twenty-six years would pass before I found myself.

Healing from abuse is a long and difficult process and is different for every survivor. My intent is not to use my journey as a model for all survivors, but to help them understand that they are not alone, and that there is a way out of the secret.

My hope is that this book will open a dialogue among those who read my story, so that victims will no longer live in the shadows. I also pray for a deeper understanding of the impact that child abuse, and particularly sexual abuse, will have on victims for the rest of their lives. This is not a wound that can heal on its own, but one that will become more infected every single day until treatment is received. Even then, the scars that are left will be deep.

Afterthoughts

Many women and men who have been subjected to severe physical or sexual abuse during childhood suffer from long-term disturbances of the psyche. They may be invaded by nightmares and flashbacks, much like survivors of war. Or conversely, they may freeze into benumbed calm in situations of extreme stress.

Dissociation and PTSD are not sharply separated and often alternate in the same individual. Dissociation, often employed by children who cannot escape from the threat of abuse, is a means of mentally withdrawing from a horrific situation by separating the event from conscious awareness. This skill allows the victim to feel detached from the body or self, as if what is happening is not happening to him or her.

Psychiatrists contend that, if repeatedly invoked in childhood, dissociation prevents memories from being integrated into consciousness and can lead to an altered sense of self. Adults may continue to use dissociation as a coping mechanism. Once dissociation or PTSD develops, the majority of psychological symptoms and the hormonal profile are very resistant to treatment.

(Reference: *Scientific American*, N.Y., (273: 4) 10/95, page 14.)

Statistics

◆ The typical child sex offender molests an average of 117 children, most of whom do not report the offense (Prevent Abuse Now, 2008).

◆ Statistics only come from reporting, so we don't have accurate, objective numbers. But based on the reports we have, 1 in 3 girls is sexually abused, and by consensus, 1 in 5 to 1 in 7 boys is sexually abused (All About Counseling, 2008).

◆ Early identification of sexual abuse victims appears to be crucial to reducing suffering of abused youth and establishing support systems for assistance in pursuing appropriate psychological development and healthier adult functioning. As long as disclosure continues to be a problem for young victims, then fear, suffering, and psychological distress will, like the secret, remain with the victim (Prevent Abuse Now, 2008).

◆ It is estimated that there are 60 million survivors of childhood sexual abuse in America today (Prevent Abuse Now, 2008).

◆ Young victims may not recognize their victimization as sexual abuse (Prevent Abuse Now, 2008).

◆ Children often fail to report due to the fear that their disclosure will bring consequences even worse than being victimized again. The victim may fear consequences from the family, feel guilt for consequences to the perpetrator, and fear subsequent retaliatory actions from the perpetrator (Prevent Abuse Now, 2008).

♦ Of 116 *confirmed* cases, a study found that 79% of the children initially denied abuse or were tentative in disclosing. Of those who did disclose, approximately three-quarters disclosed accidentally. Additionally, of those who did disclose, 22% eventually recanted their statements (Prevent Abuse Now, 2008).

References:

All About Counseling. (n.d.). Retrieved January 3, 2008, from Sexual Abuse: www.all-about- couseling.com/sexual_abuse.htm.

Prevent Abuse Now. (n.d.). Retrieved January 3, 2008, from http://www. prevent-abuse- now.com/stats.htm.

Helpful Resources

The Childhelp National Child Abuse Hotline/Voices for Children, at **800/4ACHILD (800/422-4453)** provides crisis intervention and professional counseling in English and Spanish, as well as referrals to local social services groups that offer counseling. The National Domestic Violence Hotline at **800/799-SAFE (800/799-7233) or TTY 800/787-3224** can also refer you to resources in your community, including counseling, emergency services, and assistance in reporting abuse.

Additional Resources

National Clearinghouse on Child Abuse and Neglect http://www.calib.com/ nccanch. This clearinghouse collects and publishes legal, statistical, and practical materials, many available online, about child abuse and child welfare.

Children's Council of San Francisco: Child Care Information for Parents http://www.childrenscouncil.org/parents/parents.htm. A basic overview of important issues: types of child care, how to choose a facility, what child abuse is, and what to do if you suspect abuse.

National Network for Child Care: Child Abuse Article Database http:// cyfernet.ces.ncsu.edu/cyfdb/browse_2pageAnncc.php?subcat=Abuse+and+N eglect&search;=NNCC&search;_type=browse. A helpful selection of articles with advice on recognizing abuse, preventing abuse, and understanding what an abused child is going through.

National Network for Child Care: Choosing Quality Child Care http:// www.nncc.org/Choose.Quality.Care/qual.care.page.html. Pointers on finding good child care in a center, a home-based setting, or a school. Plus articles on preparing your child for day care, and parental rights and responsibilities.

National Association of Child Care Resources and Referral Agencies http://www.childcarerr.org. Child care information for parents, child-care professionals, and child advocates.

When a Child or Youth Is Sexually Abused http://www.casat.on.ca/handindx.htm. Lengthy excerpts from a handbook for youth, parents, and caregivers. Topics include myths and facts about abuse, legal issues, emotional impact, and treatment options.

National Committee to Prevent Child Abuse http://www.childabuse.org. A resource for child abuse prevention programs in your community.

Printed in the United States
141018LV00006B/93/P